Lectio Divina

By the same author

Awake in the Spirit
Daily We Touch Him
*Centering Prayer: Renewing an Ancient
  Christian Prayer Form*
Call to the Center
Thomas Merton, My Brother
Vatican II
*In Search of True Wisdom: Visits to Eastern
  Spiritual Fathers and Mothers*
A Retreat with Thomas Merton
Praying by Hand
Lessons You Can Use from the Monastery
*Bernard of Clairvaux: A Saint's Life in Word
  and Image*
The Cistercians
Thomas Merton Brother Monk

Lectio Divina

Renewing the Ancient Practice
of Praying the Scriptures

~

M. Basil Pennington, o.c.s.o.

A Crossroad Book
The Crossroad Publishing Company
New York

The Crossroad Publishing Company
370 Lexington Avenue, New York, New York 10017

All Scripture quotations have been translated from the original languages by the author.

Printed in the United States of America

Library of Congress Cataloging-in-Publication Data

Pennington, M. Basil.
   Lectio Divina : renewing the ancient practice of praying the scriptures /
M. Basil Pennington.
     p. cm.
   Includes bibliographical references.
   ISBN 0-8245-1779-2 (hc); ISBN 0-8245-1736-9 (pbk.)
   1. Bible—Reading. 2. Bible—Devotional use. 3. Spiritual life—
Catholic Church.   I. Title.
BS617.P44 1998
248.3—DC21   97-45159
                                      CIP

5 6 7 8 9 10 02 01

For

Michael

a true Christian gentleman, a friend, a brother,

a true lover of lectio,

and

for

Grace

and all those with whom I have had the privilege

of sharing

Centering Prayer

Contents

Welcome!

Lectio, it seems to me, is a concept whose time has come. Actually, I feel a bit uncomfortable saying "concept." It is a reality, an experience that is vitalizing the lives of many today.

In fact, it is a very ancient reality. It is part of the rich heritage we received from our Jewish sisters and brothers. The accounts of Jesus' life give clear evidence that our Jewish rabbi was a man formed by lectio—from his first adventure as a man of twelve until he hung upon the cross. His first long encounter as Risen Lord with disciples was given over to sharing the fruit of his lectio, the lectio that had told him that he would die and rise again.

For the past twenty-five years we have been sharing Centering Prayer in all parts of the world. In all our prayershops we have always included lectio. For the monk and nun, lectio and contemplation, Centering Prayer, are all part of one reality. But, called to share this with women and men who do not enjoy the leisure of the cloister, we have had to package things in a practical way so that they can be more easily fitted within the demands of a home life and a life in the modern world.

When we first began our Centering Prayer pro-
grams, we found that participants were intensely
interested in the Prayer itself, in Christian "meditation," almost exclusively so. But as people have
grown in their practice, especially in the last few
years, there has been a mounting interest in lectio.
Practitioners want to know more about it, how to
enter more deeply into it, how to reap its fruits, how
to ground their contemplation more solidly through
it. The requests for workshops on lectio have poured
in from all parts of the globe. Several publishers and
many people have asked me to write this book.
Early in 1997 there was a national colloquium on
lectio in the United States. In this age of ever-
enriching interreligious dialogue, this interest in
lectio has gone out beyond the Christian community.
In July there was a very fruitful encounter between
twenty-five Catholic monastics and an equal number
of Buddhists led by the Dalai Lama, with some
hundred observers. One of the Buddhists wrote a
report on this encounter in the *Snow Lion*, a Tibetan Buddhist newspaper. The one thing he highlighted from the exchange was a paper given by a
Benedictine sister on the subject of lectio. He quoted
it at length.

What a wondrously rich heritage is ours! It begins
with the story of those days in the garden when God
walked arm-in-arm with his son Adam and his
daughter Eve and spoke intimately with this man and
his beloved wife. The whole of the rich Jewish

heritage is ours. As one of the popes put it, we are all Semites spiritually. Part of that enriching heritage is an intense love and celebration of the written Word of God.

One of the most amazing statements in the Bible—and there are lots of amazing statements in the Bible—are those words of Jesus to us: "I no longer call you servants, but friends." This is almighty God speaking, God himself, the Lord of all creation. And he says it to you and to me: "Friend."

Friend! What is more wonderful, more precious than a true friend, one who is there for us? One with whom we can share anything and everything, one with whom there is full communion and communication. Our communication with our Divine Friend needs to be a two-way street. And if we are smart, we let God get the first word in. For he surely has a lot more that is worth saying.

This is precisely what lectio, or more properly, *lectio divina* is: letting our Divine Friend speak to us through his inspired and inspiring Word. And yes, of course, it includes our response to that Word, to his communication to us through that Word. Lectio is meeting with a friend, a very special Friend who is God; listening to him, really listening; and responding, in intimate prayer and in the way we take that Word with us and let it shape our lives.

In our Christian tradition, as in all faith traditions, we have many methods of prayer and meditation. There is a bit of a problem, though, or more than one, as soon as I say "method of prayer." *Prayer* is a heavily burdened word for most of us. It carries all sorts of connotations. For many of us, praying was saying prayers and saying them right, without any "distractions." It was getting through an exercise, one due and expected, but very much a duty. No fun! It was certainly not enjoying some time with a Friend.

Does one even use a "method" when communicating with a Friend? And yet methods are helpful to us. They are there to help us do what we really want to do. The way Christians use methods for prayer and meditation is different from that found in some other traditions. In some of the traditions coming from Asia, the method used is expected to produce its own effect if it is used properly. For example, in Transcendental Meditation one uses a meaningless sound mantra until it brings about an altered state of consciousness. The Christian knows that we do not know how to pray as we ought. It is Holy Spirit who prays in us. We use a method to open the space for the Spirit to act in us freely and powerfully, to be one with us in our prayer. We use a method only insofar as it actually helps us to do what we want to do. We do not hesitate to alter it, if that is helpful, or to leave it behind when it is no longer beneficial.

If we have developed a method for our meeting with the Lord in lectio and speak about it at length, it is only that it might be helpful, that it might help us to develop the practice or habit of spending some time each day intimately with the Lord, listening to him, responding to him, growing more one in mind and heart with him and letting him practically guide us in our daily walk in this journey into the fullness of life.

The tradition of lectio is certainly one of the most ancient in the Church. It was the Word who came to us. And he formed disciples and sent them forth to bring to us all the Good News, words of life. Hearing this Good News is one of the most essential acts of our being. Receiving the Word is receiving God in a most human way: Friend to friend, sharing what is inmost. The "corporal" union with God-Christ in the Eucharist unfortunately can, like human sexual communion, stop short, on our part, with the physical or emotional—and never be a true communion of persons. When we receive the Word as word, we communicate at deeper, more fully human levels, opening the way to the divine communication that brings us into the communication within the Trinity of the Father and the Son in Holy Spirit. It is a communion beyond words because we have become one with the Word.

As I undertake to write these pages, I pray for this gift of Holy Spirit and the activity of all the gifts. And may you, too, as you enter into this little book, do the same. Then I can hope that Holy Spirit in merciful goodness will make up for all my deficiencies in writing about so basic and yet so sublime a reality as our personal intimate encounter with God in the living Word.

> —*Fr. Basil*
> St. Joseph's Abbey
> Spencer, Massachusetts

Chapter One

This Word Lectio

I hope, if it hasn't already actually taken place, that soon enough the word *lectio* will be accepted as a common word in the English language. It certainly is a word being used more and more frequently.

If you translate the word *lectio*, it means, quite simply, "reading." But lectio is much more than reading. And, in fact, we can do lectio even without having anything in front of us to read. During the first centuries of the Church and long after, most Christians could not read. Even those who could rarely owned a book. Only the wealthiest individuals or institutions, like churches and monasteries, could afford a book. The creation of a book meant the slaughter of a whole flock of sheep and thousands of hours of very specialized work. For centuries lectio was much more a matter of hearing the Word of God.

This hearing could take a number of forms.

Most commonly, a Christian would hear the Word of God in church, in the proclamation of the Word during the liturgy. The public reading was done in a set tone that would not only tell the hearers the source of the text, whether Gospel, apostolic writing, or patristic commentary, but that would also help the text to become securely lodged in the memory of the hearer.

Besides this hearing in church, those who lived in a community or associated with one could benefit from additional reading in the refectory during the course of meals, in chapter or community meetings, and in the cloister before Compline. Wealthy persons often had a cleric or secretary who would read to them, particularly at meals, but also at other times. Spiritual Fathers and Mothers would also speak the Word to their disciples.

Those who could read and had a text available to them could engage in more personal reading. For the first thousand years of the Church even this personal reading was primarily a hearing of the Word. We smile when we are told that a revered abbot like Peter the Venerable excused himself from his lectio because he had laryngitis. But for him and almost all readers of the first millennium (there were a few noted exceptions), reading meant sounding the letters inscribed on the page so that the ear could hear the words and convey them to the mind. The text was not divided into words, sentences, and paragraphs, organized to convey concepts immediately through the eye to the brain. This organized way of writing came into practice only after the middle of the twelfth century. Rather, there was a row of letters inviting the lips and the tongue to produce particular sounds. It was the *spoken word* that conveyed ideas to the mind. A cloister full of monks during their lectio was aptly spoken of as a community of mumblers.

This more complete bodily involvement had its effect on the reader. The engagement of lips and tongues, breath and ear in the reception of the Word wrote it more deeply in the person. Cadence and rhythm, such as we experience in poetry or good preaching, added to the effect. Even today, when you visit the study hall of a traditional Jewish or Muslim community you will find the students reciting the text aloud and usually swaying rhythmically as they do so. Later the same sounds and movement will accompany their meditation. When you are doing your lectio, you might try reading it aloud—not just seeing the words with your eye but speaking them with your lips and tongue and hearing them with your ear. Such reading today might not be as effective as it was in earlier times because we are usually employing a text that has been written and laid out for immediate visual transmission. However some biblical translations, especially of the Psalms, do take oral transmission into account. This fuller human experience of the Word may help us not only to retain the Word as a truly living Word but also may help us during our lectio to remain in the domain of experience.

Lectio is an experiential hearing of the Word of God. It is a hearing in the context of a certain listening. Here the faith dimension of lectio comes into play. Lectio is listening to a Person present. God lives in his Word. The Word is a Divine Presence. It may be the lips of another, the reader in church or in the Bible-sharing group, or our own lips that now pronounce the words, but it is God who speaks them, speaks them to us to be heard by us, making himself present, as any lover might, by communicating his love.

Folks with hair as white as mine may remember a usage that came from the military and became popular at the time of the Second World War. At that time, when a radio message was received in the military, if the reception was clear, the receiver would respond: "I read you." Lectio, or *lectio divina* to use its full traditional name, was in this sense "reading" God. In good lectio we "get" God's message to us. God's voice comes through to us.

Stop for a moment. Listen to all the voices around you. I don't mean the voices that might be accidentally reaching your ear from nearby speakers. I mean the hundreds of meaningful communications being beamed to you from all parts of the world. You can't hear them? Well, get out your little transistor radio and tune in. Given sufficient power and finesse in your radio, you can tune in to any message you want.

When we come to lectio empowered by faith, we tune in to the Word beamed to us by God, whether it is coming to us through the printed page before us, the voice of a reader, or the inner voice or imaginative page offered to us from memory. Since we don't have to have a book in front of us to do lectio, the blind and sight-impaired can still do lectio, as many an old monk and nun will tell you. But our inner attitude—the listening we *are*—will make all the difference in our ability to hear what God is saying to us.

Certain dispositions are indispensable and enhance our reception, making our listening able to receive the divine communication. These dispositions do not run down like the batteries in our transistor but rather grow in strength like a muscle if they are properly exercised, for like our muscle they are a gift from God, available for development with our cooperation.

∼ *Faith* ∼

First and foremost is the disposition of faith, a firm belief that the Word of God *is* the Word of God. For the full and effective reception of the communication, we believe not only that the Word who is God speaks to us through this inspired Word, but that the Word is truly present in his inspired Word and present to us as he communicates with us through the Word.

Faith enables us to find and hear the Word, one with the Father and the Spirit, in his Word. But as St. Paul told us, faith comes through hearing. Even as we faithfully hear the Word, the Word renews and strengthens our faith. This is brought about not just by hearing again of the words and deeds of God in salvation history and in the Person of Jesus and in the witness of those who saw and believed. At the deeper level, this actual experience of the Word brings us to that point where we can say with Paul: "I know in whom I believe."

∽ *Humility* ∽

An important disposition for the operation of living faith within us is *humility,* the full acceptance of reality. And the reality is that we very much need and want the divine communication. Humility is the acceptance of our profound ignorance with regard to God as well as to so many other things. We know what we know, and it is not very much. We know what we do not know, and that is a lot more. And we accept the fact that beyond this there is an infinity that we do not even know we do not know. We know that our mind and our heart, our feeling

and our emotions, our body and our soul are all a
listening, given to us by God, and that this listening
can only be filled by the Giver. We come to our
listening hungry and thirsty, filled with longing and
need. And God who is mighty does great things for
us. He fills the hungry with good things.

∼ *Openness* ∼

While an insensitivity to this need will make it difficult for us to be faithful in our regular practice of
lectio, one of the things that can most undermine
our actual practice of lectio is a subtle or not-so-
subtle boredom that seems to say: "I've heard all this
before." It is precisely the alert listening for a Real
Presence—our *openness* to all that is possible in this
moment—that forestalls this. I am not simply reading a book I have read so often before. I am meeting
a Person, a Divine Person, the God who loves me
and who has a wondrous plan for me.

Our familiarity does tend to take away the shock
that the Bible, especially the Hebrew Bible, should
be for Christians. Coming to know the God and
Father of infinite love and compassion, patience,
and mercy, the Prodigal Father revealed by Jesus
Christ, the revelation of God that we find in the early
unfolding of salvation history is certainly not what
we would expect. At least not at first thought. It
takes a bit of insight to see the God of Love lovingly

adapting himself to a very primitive people, meeting them where they are and leading them to take the next small step in faith and trust that can lead to the high moments of friendship and love that do constantly break through. One of the lessons for us to learn here is this way of Divine Love. God made us. He knows the greatest thing he has given us is our freedom, because herein lies our power to love, the source of our merit and our potential to enter into the communion of Divine Life. He does not want to overwhelm or impair this freedom. So he gently leads us, bit by bit, into the intuitions of Divine Love. No matter what the words are that we read as communications of his love, or how many times we have encountered them before, there is an opportunity for the love to expand and at the same time fill our listening for the Divine each and every time we meet our God of love in our lectio.

∾ *Faithfulness* ∾

One more essential ingredient for the true experience of lectio is a disposition of *faithfulness* to the practice. Monks and nuns in the Indian tradition wear the kavi, a very simple garment in a bright orange color—what we might call a habit. Its intense color is achieved by dipping a piece of white cotton in yellow dye a thousand times. The monastics wear this color as a reminder of their need to dip again and again into the Divine through meditation in order to attain the transformation they desire. To attain a total open listening for the Divine we need to dip again and again into the divine reading of *lectio divina*.

For our lectio to reach its full receptivity is a thing of love. It is the sensitivity of lovers that enables us to intuit more fully what the Divine Lover is seeking to convey to us through his Words of Love. Again, so obviously, we are here in a wondrous spiral. The more our love receives the intuitions of love, the more we get to know the Lover through our lectio, the more we love. This is why fidelity to lectio makes it ever more delightful—a lover exploring ever more intimately the Beloved. And we not only get to know the love and the Lover more, we get to know ourselves more as we come to see ourselves, as it were, in the eyes of the Beloved.

As powerful as all this is, there is still another whole dimension that takes us far beyond this place, infinitely so. This is the action of Holy Spirit through the gifts. As our spirit enters into a unity of spirit with the Divine Spirit of Love, we are brought into that experience of God that no eye has seen, no ear has heard—an experience that has not even entered into the loftiest concept of the human mind. Ultimately this word *lectio* describes a communication of love—a contemplative experience.

This is certainly much more than "reading." It is *lectio divina*—divine reading: reading the way the

Father "reads" the Word within the embrace that is Holy Spirit.

A statement made by Bernard of Clairvaux in one of his sermons comes to mind: "Those who have experienced this know what I am talking about. Those who have not had the experience, well, have the experience and then you will know."

Chapter Two

The Listening That We Are

At workshops and retreats I often ask participants: "Why did God make you?" A fairly fundamental question. And yet how often it catches folks by surprise—it's a question they are not aware of having seriously asked themselves, though, of course, they have been living some answer to it. Often enough I get back the catechism answer I myself learned as a boy: "God made me to know, love, and serve him in this world and to be happy with him in the next." Even as a kid I wondered how I could love God and not be happy with him right now. I think this catechism answer has probably sent more people out of the Church than any other. Pie in the sky! Serve here. Be happy there. That certainly is not our God.

God the Father and God the Son and God the Holy Spirit are and always have been among themselves a total happiness, an unending celebration of life and love. Well, when you are very happy, what do you want to do? You want to share your happiness. And multiply it! But God looked around and there was no one there to share it with. That is why God made you—and me. He wanted to have someone with whom he could share his happiness. Jesus prayed at the Last Supper: Father, I pray that they may share my joy . . . and that their joy may be complete. This is why God made us.

God is so so far beyond us. But he came to us. The Word was made flesh. Jesus is the most complete expression of the Word in our creation. God is Word. God is communication. And we therefore are essentially a *listening,* a listening for that Word. To the extent we truly "hear" that Word, receive that Word into our being and into our lives, we participate in the Divine Being, Life, Love, Joy. Made in the image of God, we have an unlimited, an infinite potential to be like unto him.

Each of us is a certain listening, a certain openness to being, to reality, to communication. Everything that has been a part of our lives since the moment of our creation has had its role in shaping the listening that we are. Objectively, of itself, the listening that we are is not good or bad, morally speaking. It just is. But it is good for us to realize that we are a certain, definable listening. It is as though my listening has a certain physical shape to it. As things come across my listening, I get only what falls within the parameters of the listening that I am.

If I am a very "set" person, very rigid in my ideas and convictions, then that is it. That is all I get, and all I will ever get. On the other hand, if I am very open person, then each thing I encounter in my "listening" has the potential to expand my listening, to push out my boundaries perhaps just a little bit more. Here is where some moral responsibility for the listening that I am does come in. It is important, in truth and in reality, that I realize and accept that I am a certain limited listening. This is humility, for humility is truth.

Indeed, it is painful to realize that in spite of our very best efforts we will still miss so much. Our listening is very limited. But let us look at the positive side. Our lectio can and will remain an inexhaustible source of enlightenment, with always more for us to receive no matter how long we have been drinking in this wonderful nectar of life. Old monks and nuns most readily bear witness to this as they lovingly caress their well-worn Bibles and struggle to receive the Word once again through thick glasses or a large magnifying glass. Each word is so precious to them.

In this humility, in this truth, then, I should want my own listening, the listening that I am, to be constantly expanded. And I should want it to be complemented by the listening of others.

One day, when I had gathered my monastic community together for a sharing, I brought in a book. I had made a special cover for the book. The front was red, the spine white, and the back green. I held the book up with the spine toward the center of the community gathering. Then I asked a monk on my left: "What color is this book?" "Red," he said with assurance. Then I asked a monk on my right. With equal assurance he declared: "Green." They were, of course, both right and both wrong. Without a shifting of their positions in the group, neither of them could approach the whole truth, except by accepting the other's "listening" or perception of reality. Together they could come to a fuller possession of the truth, yet it would still be incomplete without at least a third perspective to include the spine. This is part of the great value of meetings, of dialogue, of sharing Scripture, of shared lectio.

Our individual listening then is in part defined by our position in time and place. We do have the privilege of living in the time of the fullness of the Revelation, of living among the People of God to whom that Revelation is delivered. We have the grace of our times of being able to receive easily the Revelation in our own Bible and in other forms of the media. But far more than time and place, our listening is profoundly influenced by our attitudes, our experiences, our prejudices.

If I ask: "What is eight divided in two?" the mathematically inclined will answer without hesitation: "Four." However, someone more visually oriented might see an eight divided in the middle horizontally and say: "Two zeros." Or looking at it another way, divided vertically, might say: "Three." It is a matter of perspective, of different ways of seeing. The most basic foolishness we can be dominated by is the foolishness of self-satisfaction. All of life is a coming out of ignorance into the light of fuller understanding. For the Christian, it is getting the Easter perspective . . . and not an Easter without *Good* Friday. Life is stronger than death; good, more powerful than evil.

You bring to the reading of this book a certain listening. Your listening for this book is colored by the listening you have for the idea of lectio, your own sense of need, your aspirations. Perhaps it is formed in part by your experience of me in some workshop or through some other book I have written or by what others have told you about me. You would probably have a different listening for me if I were a woman, a lay person, a young man, a very conservative person or a very liberal one, or if I referred to God as "she." And you would be right to consider these individual characteristics, at least to some extent. For these factors would certainly color my particular presentation and the listening that *I* would have had for what I am writing about. But other factors might come in to color your listening more for what they are in themselves than for the influence they might have had on my listening. What if I were a black man, or a Jew, or a gay person?

You undoubtedly remember that day when Jesus returned to his hometown and joined the community

in the synagogue. He was asked to read. He took up
the scroll of Isaiah and read that magnificent Messianic prophecy:

> The Spirit of the Lord has been given to me,
> for he has anointed me. He has sent me to
> bring good news to the poor, to proclaim
> freedom to captives, to give sight to the blind,
> to set the oppressed free, to proclaim the time
> of the Lord's favor.

Then Jesus quietly proclaimed: "Today this prophecy
is fulfilled in your hearing."

But these people of Nazareth had a certain
listening for this man. He was Mary's boy, the
carpenter. They knew all his relatives. Their listening
for him was set, and they weren't ready to change.
When he pointed out the consequence of this
blindness, they could only rage and seek to destroy.

We each have a certain listening for Jesus of
Nazareth. We have a certain listening for God. We
most definitely bring this to our lectio—along with all
the other parameters of the listening that we are.
Jesus, on another occasion, turning again to the
prophet Isaiah, challenged his people:

> You will listen and listen again and not under-
> stand, see and see again and not perceive. For
> the heart of this nation has grown coarse, their
> ears are dull of hearing and they have shut
> their eyes for fear that they should see with

their eyes, hear with their ears, understand
with their heart and be converted and be
healed by me.

We sometimes hang on to the listening that we are,
precisely as it is here and now, because we do not
want to be converted, we do not want to change our
understanding and undertake the consequent changes
in our way of life that that would postulate. True lectio
calls not only for humility, our knowing that we have
a lot to learn, but also for a spirit of repentance, our
knowing that our ways have not been all that they
should be, and an honest desire to change . . . or
perhaps, more truly, to be changed by the Word of
God. From one end to the other, the Scriptures are
a love story. They are a Love speaking to his beloved. And we sometimes have every kind of listening for God but that of a lover. To let the Scriptures
speak to us in their nakedness can be immensely
frightening, for they demand such a love in return.

At Caesarea Philippi Jesus asked his chosen
twelve another very fundamental question: "Who do
you say that I am?" It was a moment when Peter, for
once, did not put his foot in his mouth, but shone
out in what he had to say: "You are the Christ, the
Son of the living God." Then Jesus clarified what
was actually going on: "Blessed are you, Simon bar
Jona. Flesh and blood has not revealed this to you,
but my Father who is in heaven."

So it is that another very important factor in our
listening, if we are open to it, is the activity of Holy

Spirit through the gifts. Jesus had promised that the Spirit, the Paraclete, would teach us all things. The listening that we are, because of who we are—men and women made in the image of God—can be expanded even to embrace the knowledge and experience of God himself.

With humility and gratitude those of us listening today are consoled by Jesus as surely as he consoled his listeners in Nazareth after quoting Isaiah's lament over his people:

> But happy are your eyes because they see and your ears because they hear. I tell you solemnly, many prophets and holy ones longed to see what you see and never saw it, to hear what you hear and never heard it.

In true lectio, by the power of the Word of God and of the Spirit, we do see, we do hear. The Word and the Spirit expand our listening. Their grace heals us of the binding prejudices, the fears, the selfishness and self-centeredness that would have us cling to our present parameters with the illusionary comfort of their controlled limitations. They give us the freedom to be wide open, the freedom that is rightly ours as the children of God. They lift us above all the limitations of our human reason, enabling us to be a listening not only for those transcendent truths of faith that are beyond the grasp of reason, but also for the very experience of God.

Chapter Three

Listening to the Word

Shema, Israel! Listen, O Israel!

In the beginning was the Word. And the Word was with God. And the Word was God.

Listen. Listen to a Word who is God. . . .

We really should not refer to the Hebrew Bible as the "Old Testament." No one likes to have what is most precious and very much alive to him or her called "old." The Hebrew Scriptures are not "old." Indeed, we have much to learn from our Jewish brothers and sisters in their love for the Word of God. One has only to enter a synagogue and behold the ark, above the bema, undoubtedly the focal point

19

of the whole space. With lamps burning around it, it proclaims the sacred Presence: the Word of God is here. As the sacred scrolls are brought forth for the readings, everyone who can reaches out to touch them and kiss them or at least the richly embroidered covers that protect them. The Jewish community has a wonderful feast for the celebration of the Sacred Text, when each member in turn takes the scrolls and dances with them as with a beloved.

∼ *Liturgy of the Word* ∼

For Christians, one of the most powerful experiences of hearing the Word occurs when we are gathered as the People of the Word, the People of God. Happily, in the renewal of the Church since Vatican II, the Liturgy of the Word has been restored to its proper prominence. When we gather for a Liturgy of the Word (whether celebrated on its own or as the first half of any Eucharistic celebration), we take some time to reflect on what we are about, to become more fully aware of our need for conversion and growth, and to reach out in a prayer for the divine assistance we need; we open as fully as we can to receive the Word.

Since the earliest days of the Church, Christians have prepared for the climactic moment of the proclamation of the Good News by listening to the Revelation given to the Chosen People—a reading from Hebrew Scriptures. The Hebrew Bible is God's most precious gift to his Chosen People, and we celebrate our good fortune in being heirs to this precious heritage in the Liturgy of the Word. Though looking to a new fullness in the coming of the Anointed One, the Hebrew Scriptures remain ever new, alive, fresh, full of life, and life-giving as the Word of God.

Sometimes, too, our minds and our hearts are prepared for the proclamation of the Good News by the words of one of the men who knew Jesus personally, loved him intimately, and was inspired by Holy Spirit to share his insight with the churches. Thus, a reading from the Christian Scriptures, the "New Testament," might be included—something from the letters of Paul or Peter or the Acts of the Apostles.

We respond to this preparatory word with reflection and prayer, rising to a new level of celebration in the Alleluias that precede the proclamation of the Gospel. We ourselves rise and stand at attention. The Sacred Text is carried to the lectern. Traditionally this Sacred Book is richly adorned, a tradition still very much alive among our Orthodox brothers and sisters, bespeaking something of the richness that lies within. Candles, sacred lights, sometimes accompany the Text; clouds of incense, too, that bring to mind the great moments of theophany. This is a most solemn moment. The one who is privileged to proclaim this Word prays over us: "The

Lord be with you." And we in turn pray over him: "And with your spirit."

As he opens the proclamation: "The Holy Gospel according to . . . ," we cry out: "Glory to you, O Lord!" It is as though the bearer has disappeared, and it is the Lord himself who now proclaims his Good News. "Praise to you, Lord Jesus Christ!" It is a *proclamation*, not a simple reading. The Gospel is always and in every part a proclamation of the Resurrection—a shout of joy even in its darkest parts. It needs to be always heard in this light, the radiant light of the Risen Lord.

We bring to this most graced moment the listening that we are. But we want to be as open as we possibly can be, to welcome this Word and allow it to inform, expand, and transform the listening that we are.

Now Mother Church, who serves up this rich meal, is a good Jewish mama. If you have ever been a guest in a Jewish home, you know how it is. Mama sits next to you, and each time you take one spoonful from your plate, Mama adds two more. It is too much! I have had a difficulty here. I have found that if I try to grasp all that is served up at the Liturgy of the Word, it all seems to run through my fingers. So what I now do in practice is to choose one small tasty morsel. Sometimes one particular nugget is given to me—one word, sentence, or phrase strikes me very forcefully; at other times, I select one. In any case, I take away from the Liturgy of the Word a "word of life," which I talk over with the Lord after Communion and carry with me through the day. I allow the word to re-echo in my mind and in my heart, giving color to all that I experience through the day.

~ *Sharing the Word* ~

This community gathering for the celebration of the Liturgy of the Word is a privileged place for receiving the Word that builds faith. But wherever two or three are gathered in his name, there he is in the midst. Each of us is a Christ, baptized into Christ, able to speak most authentically the Word of salvation. We can share the Word with one another—sometimes even more intimately and more fruitfully than we can glean from either our own private efforts or a more formal proclamation and explanation—not only in organized faith-sharing or Bible-sharing groups but also in informal moments around the dinner table, over a cup of coffee, or while waiting in the check-out line. Indeed, there is no place that our faith cannot shine out, if we let it. We certainly do not need to charge others with it, like some warring crusader. That would not be respectful or loving. But there is always room for a loving, caring sharing in all our human contacts, even if it is not voiced in words. And to the extent we receive the shared word, that we truly "hear" it, faith is built up in us.

∼ *Sacred Reading* ∼

Although we cannot always be with others, at least physically, we can always let the Word speak to us. The most common way is by means of the printed word, as we take our Bible in hand and in heart. These days, though, it can almost as easily be by technological means—video or audio cassettes or the Internet. However we choose to access Scripture, there are three different approaches that we need in our lives.

SACRED STUDY

The Lord has given us humans a most wonderful gift—a mind that is capable of abstracting ideas and forming concepts, that can think and reflect, analyze and synthesize. And God has given us the primary command, which bespeaks the most fundamental aspiration of our being: "Love the Lord your God with your whole mind." We must ever press our edges, ever seek to use our minds to their fullest. Feeding the mind and developing our intellectual understanding of God's Word is crucial to our spiritual development. Thus sacred study needs to be a regular part of every Christian's life, whether through Bible study or in those other disciplines that help us to receive the Revelation more fully.

It is a great help if we can belong to a study group that meets regularly. Such support and accountability will keep us going, while the shared insights of the members will make our study richer and more exciting.

But each of us will have to program time for this study into our lives and find the level of study that best serves us. For some, the teaching columns of the diocesan newspaper or some good magazine may be enough, provided they aren't too narrow or slanted in perspective. Others will need a more meaty fare, something they can really chew, from which they can get the nourishment they need.

For some who are gifted in this area, the study of the biblical languages can be fruitful. One of the more famous Christian teachers in Japan today is Father Oshida. He was raised a Buddhist and became a Christian in his late teens. He entered the Dominican order and prepared for the priesthood. When he began studying scholastic theology he got such headaches that he began sitting zazen, which he had never done as a Buddhist. But it was when he studied Hebrew and began to be able to receive the Word in its original Hebrew—and to experience even the Greek texts in the light of the Hebrew— that he really heard the Word as a Japanese person. No longer was it filtered to him through the listening of Western minds in translations. There is an old saying: "Every translator is a traitor." Certainly the listening of the translator profoundly affects the text he or she delivers to us. Moreover, the cluster of nuances that embraced and enriched the original word are left behind and the new word has its own collection, which deeply colors what we receive. So language study can certainly open the way for us to a whole new listening for the Word of God.

MOTIVATIONAL READING

But no matter how complete, rich, and full our reception of the Word of God, it does not become a part of our lives if we do not live it. It must be embraced by mind *and* heart. We are to love the Lord our God "with our whole mind, our whole heart, . . . " This affective and effective embrace of the Good News often needs the energy and support of motivational reading. This is what I think most people mean when they speak of "spiritual read-ing"—the reading that motivates us to open to the Spirit and receive the grace we need to live up to what we know. Unlike sacred study, such reading may not need to be regular. Many other things can motivate us. Certainly the events of everyday life often put us deeply in touch with our fragility, fallibility, and need, and turn us to God, to faith, and to hope. Motivational reading may be more neces-sary in particular areas of our faith journey. Perhaps we are finding that the Mass is no longer very meaningful to us, or we are having difficulty praying, or the value of chastity is extremely challenged. It is time to seek support and enlightenment in the faith sharing of others through their writings, relying on Holy Spirit to make what they share come alive in us.

Lectio Divina

Lectio can certainly be a source of faith-building, enlightening the mind as much as any study and motivating the will through powerful impulses of love. But neither of these is primary in lectio. We come to lectio not so much seeking ideas, concepts, insights, or even motivating graces; we come to lectio seeking God himself and nothing less than God. We come seeking the experience of the presence of the living God, to be with him and to allow him to be with us in whatever way he wishes. It is a time for listening: "Speak, Lord, your servant wants to hear." It is an active listening, or interactive, as they might say today. We engage the received Word with who we are today and what is going on in our lives today. But it is *listening,* giving the Lord the first word and letting that word expand our listening. It is difficult for us, but it is important, extremely important, that in lectio we do not try to contract the Word we receive to the dimensions of our already-held concepts and ideas. Rather, it is necessary to allow those ideas to be blown open, if need be, to give space to the received Word. We do not want to truncate the divine communication to the narrow confines of our presently held concepts. Instead, we want the Word to expand our receptivity, our listening, to allow space for more and more of the divine wisdom, knowledge, and understanding. Lectio is essentially prayer at a deep experiential level.

We Christians share with our Jewish brothers and sisters the immense privilege of being sons and daughters of the Book. In saying this I certainly do not want to deny that God in some way speaks through the sacred writings of other traditions. The wisdom of a Confucius, limited though it is to the rational level, has a truth about it that must be guided by the Truth. The wisdom found in some of the writings of ancient India, albeit mixed at times with some fanciful mythology, must have its source in the divine Wisdom. Not a few of the truths of our Book are re-echoed, if not actually reproduced, in the pages of the Qur'an. But the fact remains that the Bible is a book wholly inspired by God, who guided the writers, gracefully in accord with their freedom and God-given gifts, to express only what God wanted them to express and all that God wanted them to write in his name. The Bible is a most precious gift of the Lord, given through human minds, hearts, and hands, a special depository of the Revelation-bearing Tradition. It is the divinely inspired Word of God.

So it is, we might say, "natural" for us to go first of all to the Bible to listen to the Word. But it is also true: "Through him all things were made." The whole of the creation bespeaks its Maker. As the Greeks would say, the whole of creation is full of *logoi*, "little words," that give expression to the *Logos*, the Word. I can stand on my bluff overlooking the Pearl River Delta and wonder at it all: the creation of God and humans, the beauty of the sky, the sea, and the islands, the exuberant energy of metropolis Hong Kong—it all speaks of God, gives expression to the Word. I can look upon the form and figure of a person, the wonder of a human body, the beauty of a human face, and know that God became a man and that God expresses himself in the beauty and nobility of every man and woman and child. I listen to the Word of God crying out in the degradation of the addict huddling in his filthy rags in the doorway of an alley, and my heart cries with the Word. Basking in the serene goodness of friendship, I hear the longings of the Word in my regard.

As the inspired poet sang:

> The heavens shout forth the glory of God,
>> the vault of heaven proclaims his handi-
>>> work.
> Day tells of it to day,
>> night to night hands on the word.
> No speech at all, no word,
>> no sound that anyone can hear,
> Yet their voice goes out through all the world,
>> their message to the ends of the earth.
>>>>> —Psalm 19

Yes, all that the Word has made and keeps on making bespeaks the Word and is to be heard, if we have but the listening. But still, among all these words, we are gifted with that most precious and direct communication of the inspired Word of God.

We turn to it in particular to hear. In speaking to the bishops of Italy, the Holy Father recently lamented, "There are too many faithful who remain deprived of a vital encounter with sacred Scripture and who fail to nourish their faith with the richness of the Word of God." He then set an example for the other bishops by rising from his sickbed in the first days of Lent to begin personally the distribution of a million Bibles to the people of his diocese.

It is in the Word of God that we can most readily hear the Word of God. It is the Word of God that can most powerfully expand our listening for the Word of God wherever he speaks to us. My confrere, Thomas Merton, expressed this beautifully:

> By the reading of the Scripture I am so re-newed that all nature seems renewed around me and with me. The sky seems to be a purer, a cooler blue, the trees a deeper green, light is sharper on the outlines of the forest and the hills, and the whole world is charged with the glory of God and I find fire and music in the earth under my feet.

Chapter Four

A New Packaging

Morning after morning he opens my ear that I
may hear.

—Isaiah the Prophet

The reason for the popularity of many of the teachers of meditation who came to the United States from India and other Asian countries was that their teaching was very simple and precise. They gave the seeker a method that could immediately be put into practice.

Likewise, one of the reasons the rosary is so popular is that it is the one prayer method that *we* have been teaching in a very concrete and practical way. We place a set of prayer beads in the hands of the learner and then tell him or her precisely how to proceed: Say this prayer here, this prayer here, this prayer here, and while you are saying these prayers, reflect on these events in the saving action of our blessed Lord. People can learn the rosary method without difficulty, and they begin immediately to put it into regular practice. It certainly is an excellent prayer form, open to many levels of communication between the pray-er and the Lord. I have published a couple of books exploring the richness of this form of prayer.

Apart from the rosary and the Stations of the Cross, a devotion that requires a particular place for practice, we have rarely taught our methods of prayer in simple, practical ways that the learner can immediately begin to use. I would like to present a very simple, practical method of lectio that anyone can easily follow and instantly put into practice.

Let me first spell out the method very precisely; then I will explain the elements a bit.

∼ *Lectio Divina* ∼

1. *Come into the Presence and call upon Holy Spirit.*
2. *Listen for ten minutes to the Lord speaking to you through the Sacred Text.*
3. *Thank the Lord and take a "word."*

Our Bible should be one of our most treasured possessions. We don't want to just leave it on the desk or put it on the shelf with other books. Rather, we want to enthrone it in our home, in our room, in our office. (In Appendix Three you will find a simple rite for enthroning the Bible in the home.) The Bible bespeaks a Real Presence, a place where we can encounter the living God whenever we will.

When it comes time for our lectio, we pick up our book with reverence. For just a moment we reflect on the wonder of the Divine Reality, present here in his Word in this book in our hands. And we turn to Holy Spirit. This Word is so special because Holy Spirit in a very special way inspired these writers to write all and only what God wanted to use to communicate with us. As our Lord told us at the Last Supper, Holy Spirit abides with us to teach us all things, bringing to mind all that he has taught us. So we ask Holy Spirit, who inspired these texts and who abides within us as teacher, to make them now a living communication with the Lord, to help us to understand all that the Lord now wants to communicate to us.

I have drawn this little method largely from a book of usages or spiritual practices from the year 1132. As we are in a living tradition, this book in its turn depends on earlier practice. In this book of usages, the author spells out the entrance into lectio, producing almost a liturgy: We take the book with reverence and kneel down. We call upon Holy Spirit for help. Then we listen to the first words on our knees and kiss the text, and only then do we sit down to continue our lectio. Such an elaborate liturgy might not suit us well today in our own lives, but it probably would help us to have some little ritual of our own for coming into the Divine Presence and invoking the aid of the Spirit.

We then listen for a designated amount of time. We *listen*. We don't just read. The Lord is present, speaking to us. We listen to him. And we respond.

When I was sharing Centering Prayer in Korea a couple of years ago, I saw a cartoon that I liked. It showed a flight of steps that went up and up and up. A little man stood on the top step. In front of him was a great big ear. This, I fear, is how many people think of prayer: ascending on high we pour out our troubles and our needs into the ear of God. I don't think anyone, even God, likes a one-way conversation. In lectio we have the wisdom not only to give God a chance to say something to us, but to let him speak first and give direction to our conversation.

It is best to determine the duration of our lectio by a set time. If we say we will read a page or a chapter, we are so ordered to getting things done that there will be a real push from within to get to the end of the page or chapter. But if we have decided we are just going to sit here with the Lord for these few minutes, then we can receive the Word with a certain openness and sense of leisure. If the first word or the first sentence speaks to us, we can just sit with it, let it come alive within us, respond to it. There is no need to push on. The rest of the text will be there for tomorrow's encounter.

It is good to set a fairly short time for ourselves, something we can fit easily into each day. The Lord can say a lot to us in two minutes, if he wants to. If we choose a short time, we are more apt to be faithful to a daily meeting with the Lord in his Word. Even if we find ourselves at the end of a very full day and have not yet made time for our lectio, we can take two minutes or five minutes to sit with the Lord before crawling into bed. And certainly there would be nothing to forbid our prolonging the time whenever the leisure is available to us.

Before I came to China I spent a few years in our monastery in the Ozarks. This is one of the poorest areas in the United States. The people living in these mountains are very poor but often very devout. I found among the people there a very good practice. Do you know where they enthrone their Bible? On the pillow on their bed. This means that when they go to bed, they have to pick up their Bible. And they take a moment to get a word from the Lord to carry with them into sleep. Then they place the Bible on their shoes. In the morning, of course, when they rise, they have to pick up the Bible. And again they receive a word from the Lord to carry with them through the day. Clever people, those friends in the mountains.

When it is time to conclude this particular meeting with the Lord, we thank him and take a "word" —a word or a sentence or a phrase—with us.

Taking time to thank the Lord follows from our sense of his very real presence and reinforces this belief. And it is most appropriate. If we want to talk with the pastor, we usually have to go chasing after him. If we want to talk to the bishop, we have to make an appointment. If we want to talk to the pope, well, we have to pull a few strings. But if we want to talk to almighty God, we can just sit down and open our Bible and there he is, ready to talk with us! We are indeed privileged: *whenever we want,* we can sit with our Lord!

Near our monastery in Spencer, Massachusetts, we have over the years acquired a number of new neighbors. Off in one direction there is an Insight Meditation Center. In another there is an ashram. And then there are the Tibetan Buddhists. Happily, we have very good relations with these brothers and sisters. In that area a very large percentage of the people are Christian. Sad to say, there is no Christian meditation center, so many of those who go to these centers near us are Christians. And our friends welcome us to their centers to help Christians integrate the new methods of meditation they are learning into their own faith context.

Every once in a while, I used to sense a certain excitement creeping into the environment. Soon I would hear: "Swamiji is coming." "Achincha is

coming." Our friends would be excited that soon
they would have an opportunity to sit at the feet of
their master for a few days and drink in his teaching.
They would always invite us to come to hear their
master or ask to bring the master to our monastery
to visit with us. At those moments the thought
always came to me: It is my Master who made those
masters, and I can sit at his feet any time I want. I
have only to open my Bible.

Our Order has an ashram high in the mountains
in Kerela in southwest India, among the people
brought to the faith by St. Thomas the Apostle.
Once when I was visiting the monks there, I met a
wonderful old Christian swami. When this venerable
old man, now near a hundred years old, was nine-
teen, he conceived of the idea of being a Christian
swami. That was a few years ago, and at that time
there was little thought of such an idea and less
tolerance for it. Nonetheless, he pursued his idea,
received the kavi from his father, and set forth on
what was a very traditional life for a swami. During
the dry season he traveled around, telling all about
his Guru, the Lord Jesus, and sharing Jesus' teaching with them, eating whatever was given to him and
sleeping in whatever temple or ashram was at hand.
When the wet season came, he would find some
monastery or convent that would take him in, and
he would spend his time studying the teaching of his
Master. After he had been doing this for over fifty
years, he came upon our ashram in Kerela. A whole

community of Christian swamis—what a joy! It became a home for him, though he continued for the most part his traditional life.

I am told that at the end of the teaching season, before the rains come, many swamis gather at one of the great shrines for some days of sharing. And often our swami is in their midst. When he is there, on the last day of the gathering, he will climb to the platform, certainly a most venerable and venerated figure. And he always begins his sharing with his fellow swamis in the same way: I have the supreme, exalted, and sublime privilege of being the disciple of the Sat-Guru, the Guru of gurus, Jesus Christ! And then he goes on to tell them about Jesus and his teaching. This I know: In all my years of travel and teaching I have never met anyone who has had such a sense of the wonderful privilege it is to be a disciple of Jesus Christ as this venerable old man. And that privilege is our privilege. We can each day sit at the feet of our Master and receive from him a word of life.

We thank the Lord, indeed. And we take a "word" with us. Some days we hardly need take a word, for one is clearly given to us. I am sure most of those reading this book will have had the experience of being with the Lord in the Word and suddenly a word truly comes alive.

There is one instance of this that stands out clearly in my mind. One day many years ago I was doing my lectio. I was at the beginning of the Gospel of St. Matthew. You know how that goes: "Abraham begot Isaac, Isaac begot Jacob, . . . " I stopped and spoke to the Lord: "I know you are a good Jew and all this genealogy stuff means a lot to you, but what are you trying to say to me?" He didn't say anything. So I read on: "Jesse begot David, David begot Solomon, . . . " Again I stopped: "Lord, what are you trying to say to me with all this 'begot, begot' stuff?" But he didn't seem to say anything, so I read on. Three times fourteen generations. Finally I came to: "Jacob begot Joseph the husband of Mary, from whom was born Christ the Lord." And at that moment the Lord "spoke" that word to me. I knew then as I had never known before that my God had gotten into my flesh, that my God was once a young man just my age. I had heard that Gospel many times in the liturgy. I had read it many times before on my own. But that particular day the Lord spoke that word to me, and it changed my life. Some days it's that clear and undeniable.

Other days we are not so blessed. Indeed, it sometimes seems as though the Lord has not shown up. So, at the end of our lectio time, we ourselves have to take the initiative to choose a word to carry with us. Often, later in the day, that word will come to life for us; or it may prove to be just the word someone else needs.

There is a wonderful Easter sermon of Guerric of Igny, a twelfth-century Cistercian abbot. He is commenting on the Gospel passage that relates the story of the three women coming to the tomb and finding it empty. As they retrace their steps, they meet the Lord on the way. Guerric says to the brothers: "You know how it is, my dear brothers. Some days we go to our lectio, and the Lord doesn't seem to show up. We go on to the liturgy, and he is seemingly nowhere around. We approach the tomb of the altar, and it seems completely empty. Then as we go down the garden path on our way to work, lo—suddenly there is the Lord."

The first time I heard this sermon it really spoke to me because of an experience I had had in my first days in the monastery. In those days we had very strict rules of silence. We could only speak to the abbot and the novice master. But for the first month that we were in the monastery we continued to wear our lay clothing, so that everyone knew we were stupid postulants and we could get away with anything (though we didn't know that!). As I was coming in from work on my third day in the monastery, I ran into Father William. I then thought of him as one of the venerable seniors. He died some forty years later, indeed one of the venerable seniors. Father William was coming in from the garden and tears were running down his cheeks. Being the impetuous postulant that I was, I forgot all about the rule of silence and ran up to Father: "Are you all right, Father?" Father had the benignity to set aside the rules for this stupid postulant: "Yes, I am fine. I was out in the greenhouse, puttying the windows. And as

I worked, suddenly my word came alive and grew and grew and grew until I was totally enveloped in the Divine Love. And all I could do was cry." And he added, with that wonderful simplicity that was his: "It was difficult to finish puttying the windows with all those tears in the way."

This very simple little practice of each day meeting the Lord in his Word and receiving from him a word of life can indeed transform our lives. If each day we can take a word from our lectio and it comes alive for us and forms our mind and heart, we will indeed come to have the mind and heart of Christ.

∿ *Liturgy of the Hours* ∿

In recent years many Christians have taken to praying the Liturgy of the Hours. This method of prayer has a certain preeminence as being in a special way the prayer of the Church. In this prayer we, his People, join in a special way with Christ as our Head and Mediator to bring to the Father the honor and praise that are his due and to cry out for all the needs of the People of God and for our world. Traditionally, the Church has asked those who have been united in a special way with Christ in his mediatorial office through ordination into the ministerial priesthood to be faithful in entering into this way of prayer each day. Those, too, who have responded to Christ's invitation to consecrate their

lives to intimacy with him through the profession of
the evangelical counsels have been asked faithfully to
take part in this prayer of Christ and his Church. But
with the renewal and a deeper awareness of the
universal call to holiness among the People of God,
many of the faithful now join priests and religious in
this way of prayer.

Under the powerful influence of the Spirit, the
Liturgy of the Hours has been renewed, better
adapting to the lives of those who are fully engaged
in the activities of Church and secular society,
leaving with the monks and nuns the form that
originated with them and for their way of life. The
Liturgy of the Hours now consists of a Morning
Prayer and an Evening Prayer, with a short Day
Prayer that can be placed where it is most appropriate, and a short completing prayer, Compline, for
the end of the day. Then there is the Office of
Readings. This is precisely an office of lectio.

It certainly should not surprise us to find an office
of lectio in the Liturgy of the Hours. It is fundamentally important to keep in mind that the Liturgy of
the Hours is a *method of prayer.* We have seen that
prayer, communication and communion with God,
must be a two-way street. There must be a time for
listening as well as for speaking. And a wise person
will first listen when the "Other Party" is the All-
Wise. Traditionally, what is now called the Office of
Readings was called Vigils. It was often celebrated
the night before or very early in the morning while it

was still the night. St. Benedict provided that it should be prayed an hour or so after midnight. Cistercians (Trappists), who seek to live the Rule of Benedict in its fullness, usually rise around 3:00 A.M. for this Office. Such a timetable does not usually fit readily into the life of a person living an active life in the world today. So with the renewal of the Liturgy of the Hours, this Office is now called what it truly is, an Office of Readings; it can be celebrated at whatever time best suits the pray-er.

Since the Liturgy of the Hours is a method of prayer, it is constructed to help us to pray. There is no great merit in just reading all the words in the book or "saying" the Office. Priests who have viewed the Liturgy, or the breviary, as it was called, in this way rarely found it sufficiently meaningful to be faithful to it. If they were, it was often experienced more as a penance than as a refreshing prayer, a time of intimate, loving communion with the God whom they loved and who loved them.

For those who commit themselves to praying the Liturgy of the Hours, the Office of Readings is their daily lectio. And this particular Office can best be approached in this way. The opening prayers of the Office are a cry for divine assistance, a calling upon the Spirit. The psalmody that follows is an opportunity to quiet our spirit and really come into the Divine Presence. The psalms allow us to leave behind the cares and doings we have been engaged in, to free ourselves and to open ourselves to listen truly now and to hear what the Lord has to say to us today.

As we enter into listening to the readings that the Church has chosen for us today, it is good for us to establish for ourselves a reasonable time to spend with the Office of Readings. We might even go further and decide how much time we will spend with the preparatory psalmody and how much time with the actual readings. This way, if some verse of the day's psalms really speaks to us and invites us to enter into deeper communion with God for a bit, we can do so either within the limits of the determined time or for a longer period if we are able to free ourselves for it. Remember, the Liturgy of the Hours is a method of *prayer*. It is not a question of reading so much text. It is a question of using the text provided to help us really pray. If on a particular day we do not need all the given text, or need very little of it, to enter into very real prayer for and with Christ and our Church, then there is no great value in reading all the text. Indeed, to push on, reading instead of entering into deeper prayer, is to miss the whole meaning of what the Church is asking us to do. So we set, let us say, five minutes for the psalmody, and we pray the psalms for that amount of time, whether we use one verse, twenty verses, or all the verses printed in the book for that particular day. We pray the psalms for the time we can and do rightly allot to this particular preparation for our listening.

Then we move on to the readings. And here again, we have set a time since there is no push to get through a certain amount of text. What we want to do is to be with the Lord, to listen to him, and to hear what he has to say to us today. If he gives us an ear-full and a heart-full in the first sentence, we stay with it. We let it speak to our deepest being, reform our listening, call forth a total response, refresh and renew us, give us a "word of life" to take with us as we return to our daily tasks and ministry. There is no need to push on and read every word that is printed there. They will be there next year and the year after. They will speak to us or the Lord will speak to us through them in due time. Let us not miss what he is saying to us today. And let that word really take root in us, let it be deeply rooted in good soil. Let us get a "word of life" that will bring a new liveliness to all the rest of the day, to our praying of the other hours, to our being with our sisters and our brothers as the Christ person that we are.

For those, then, who pray with the Church the Liturgy of the Hours, lectio is not an add-on, one more thing to fit into our perhaps already overly full day. Lectio is an integral part of the Liturgy of the Hours, the Office of Readings, which nourishes us and prepares us to pray all the other hours well.

Chapter Five

Father/Mother, Give Me a Word of Life

Lectio has been an essential part of Christian life since it first emerged within the Jewish community. As the fourth century unfolded, it seemed that Christianity was finally gaining some respectability. And yet in this same fourth century, to many in the Mediterranean area it seemed as if the whole fabric of society was coming apart. The Empire was splitting in two as barbarian hordes threatened it on every side. Which threatened Christian life more: its newfound respectability or the barbarian? It would be hard to say. The Founder's dictum to "render unto Caesar the things that are Caesar's and unto God the things that are God's" was more and more difficult to follow as taxes soared, ever-increasing military service was demanded, and a worldly Christianity began to flourish at the court and elsewhere in the Empire.

It is not surprising, then, that the desert began to receive devout Christians, inspired by the example of the Baptizer—of whom "there was none greater born of woman"—and of the Master himself, who spent forty days in the desert before he began his public ministry.

When the young Alexandrine, Anthony, heard afresh the words, "Go, sell what you have and follow me," he did just that. First he disposed of the greater part of his wealth, saving only a portion to insure care for his sister, and withdrew to the outer edges of the city. But again the evangelical word resounded in his soul and he sold all, placed his sister in competent hands, and went forth into the desert. He was not the first there. He encountered the ancient Paul, but Patriarch Athanasius's *Life of Anthony* led to his being the most influential example. Thus we see that it was a word received in lectio that is credited with giving birth to a powerful spiritual movement.

As the fourth century progressed, the desert became increasingly peopled by hermits, who often grouped themselves in loosely connected associations, and then by cenobites, who lived in organized communities, often guided by the rules developed by the saintly Pachomius. Besides the many who went to the desert to settle there, the latter part of the

century began to see a steady flow of pilgrims
seeking to be edified by immediate contact with
these already fabled saints as well as to partake of
their wisdom. These pilgrims not only wrote accounts of their journeys, giving us many colorful
details with regard to the lives of the Fathers and
Mothers of the Desert, but men like John Cassian
sought to retell their wisdom in collections of
conferences and sayings.

The wisdom of the desert enshrined in these
variegated writings continued to flow through western Christian life even during what has been called
the Dark Ages, and it shed a strong light on the
renaissance the Church experienced as it moved into
the glorious twelfth century. But with the Last of the
Fathers, Bernard of Clairvaux, and his contemporar-
ies, the patristic age came to a close. A scholastic
era, perhaps drier than the deserts of the Fathers,
began to hold sway. There were moments when the
Desert Fathers were heard again, as with de Rancé
in the seventeenth century, but for the most part this
wisdom lay dormant during the whole of the scholastic parenthesis. With the inspired renewal of our
century, welcoming again the full humanism of the
patristic age, there is a listening once again receptive
to the wisdom of the desert.

At first one might feel that the heroic ways of
these desert giants is too far removed from the quest
of the everyday seeker living in this world's society.
However, the Fathers and Mothers themselves,

along with their early historians, sought to make it
clear to us that this is not the case. Noteworthy in
this regard is the rather lengthy account in the
History of the Monks of Egypt of the last days of
the fabled Abba Paphnutius. We are told that as his
end approached, he "entreated the Lord to show
him his like upon earth." And whom did the Lord
show the saintly Father? A street musician who had
been a thief, the very busy headman of a local
village, and a wealthy Alexandrine merchant. As the
priests gathered around the dying saint, he told them

> all that the Lord had revealed to him, saying to
> them that no one in this world ought to be
> despised, let him be a thief, or an actor on the
> stage, or one that tilled the ground and was
> bound to a wife, or was a merchant and served
> a trade: for in every condition of human life
> there are souls that please God and have their
> hidden deeds wherein he takes delight; whence
> is it plain that it is not so much profession or
> habit that is pleasing to God as the sincerity
> and affection of soul and honesty of deed. And
> when he had spoken thus about each in turn,
> he gave up his spirit.

The final word of a great and saintly Father. No
teaching could be given greater emphasis.

Everyone baptized into Christ, every true seeker,
is called to the freedom of the children of God. And

this was essentially the quest of the desert: free-dom—to be free to be oneself, to be who we truly are, to celebrate our oneness in our common human-ity and in our call to share in the bliss of the divinity.

What is most evident and distinctive about these Fathers and Mothers is that they went apart, that they shunned a society that set its values in the goods of this world and in prestige in their transient universe. Most of us cannot go apart so radically, but we do need to separate ourselves from enslavement to this world's values. We may have to be in the world, but we cannot be of the world. Yes, render unto Caesar the things that are Caesar's, but render unto God, as fully and completely as we can, the things that are God's. This is the most clear witness of the men and women who fled from an increas-ingly worldly Church to the freedom of the desert.

This is not easy. Even if we were to spend as much time at the Lord's feet in the Scriptures as we do before the TV enthroned in our homes, of itself it would be a losing battle. For the TV is armed by the masters of the art of persuasion and all the sophisti-cation of the ever-more-modern media, and it calls forth as its ally the incalculable pressure of our peers to win us over to its hierarchy of values. It is only by the powerful grace of the Spirit that the Word of God, a double-edged sword, can pierce through and separate our spirit from the clutches of the worldly spirit. And that Holy Spirit will operate within as a liberating force only if we seek and welcome her.

We need to carve out some time apart for ourselves to escape from the bombardment of the world
and to come to our true self. Our place apart can be
a corner of our room where our Bible proclaims a
Presence. Our going apart may be just turning our
chair away from our desk with all its affairs, leaving
the world behind for a few minutes while we rest in
the Presence and know ourselves to be held in a
great and tender love. Or we may find our going
apart to be found in a short walk to a church, a
library, or a park, some quiet spot where we can sit
for a bit in the quietness and know something of the
quies of the desert.

Quies, quiet—that wonderful freedom to be able
to rest quietly in the Lord, knowing that in him we
have all. No longer tugged this way and that by our
passions, emotions, uncontrolled desires—this is
what was behind all the austerity of the desert, what
motivated it, and what encouraged the monks and
nuns to persevere in it. They longed for the freedom
to do what they really wanted to do, be who they
wanted to be, without having to struggle constantly
against thoughts—which for them included also all
fantasies and feelings—that sought to master them
and rule them. This freedom is essential if we are
going to be able to hear the Lord in our lectio.

We cannot hope to free ourselves from the false
self that the values of this world encourages us to
create, to escape the self-alienation that marks our
lives from the womb and is constantly fostered by a

worldly society, if we do not at times and even
regularly seek periods of quietness. This is the goal
of all authentic meditation practices and especially of
that centering prayer that comes to us from this
desert tradition—the quietness that enables us to be
Christ to the Father in Holy Spirit.

But anyone who has practiced meditation knows
that the asceticism of the practice lies not only in
giving time to meditation, but in managing during
the actual time of meditation to be faithful in setting
aside thoughts, feelings, emotions, desires, all the
expressions of the self. Herein is the true purpose of
ascetic practice: to free ourselves from the imperious
domination of our own thoughts, passions, and
desires, to free the spirit for the things of the Spirit.
It is paradoxical, isn't it, that what seem to be life-
denying practices actually open the space for new
life? The men and women of the desert, who all but
died to life in this world, found the way, already here
and now, to enter into some participation of eternal
life, with its joy beyond earthly joy. These holy ones
were largely skilled in hiding these more sublime
workings of God within them, but between the lines
and in the candid instructions to beloved disciples we
catch glimmers of the fullness of life that they experienced. They certainly give witness to the reality of a
life beyond this life—a fuller, richer, happier life.
They tell us, more by the way they lived than by
their wonderful words, that this life is to be lived
more for that life than for this one.

The "sayings of the Fathers," those rough-hewn words of life or words of salvation, can cut ruthlessly through all our pretenses. And that is good. They are far more precious than the sometimes starry-eyed, always colored accounts of the pilgrims and storytellers. These words are very nearly if not the actual words that passed through the desert wastes from the lips of one disciple to another, once they fell from the lips of some revered Father or Mother. Their rough angularity has its audacious way of intruding with a cutting edge into some of our most sacred preserves. As the great Barsanufius wrote to Archimanrite Dorotheos: "For those capable of understanding these words and keeping them, there is joy and great profit." An eagerness for a "word of life" should mark every Christian. We can with great profit turn to the sayings of the Fathers and Mothers of the Desert. But like the Fathers and Mothers themselves, we need more fundamentally to turn to their ever-fruitful source, the Holy Scriptures. The author of the *History of the Monks of Egypt,* with perhaps a bit of enthusiastic exaggeration, tells of the monks' and nuns' eagerness in this regard: "And nowhere have I seen such meditation on Holy Writ or understanding of it, or such discipline of sacred learning; well-nigh might you judge each one of them a doctor in the wisdom of God." A daily meeting with the Lord in the Gospels, as a true disciple seeking a word of life from the Master, is the surest way for each one of us to grow into the mind of Christ.

When seekers came to the desert, they approached a Father or Mother and quite simply asked for "a word of life." And the Father or Mother would most often give the seeker a word from the Scriptures, sometimes elaborating upon the power of such a word. We might give a classic example of this from the pages of the *Conferences* of St. John Cassian. Perhaps no writings coming from the desert have been more influential since Benedict of Nursia, the great monastic legislator of the West, provided all his monks the opportunity to become thoroughly familiar with these conferences. In his *Tenth Conference*, St. John tells us how he and his companion, Germanus, approached the man who was reputed to be at that time the holiest, oldest, and wisest Father of the Desert. In seeking a word of life they had asked him specifically for a word on prayer. Abba Isaac responded to them most generously:

> I must give you a word for contemplation. If you dutifully keep this word before you and learn to recollect it at all times, it will help you to mount to contemplation of high truth. . . . The word is this: "O God, come to my assistance. O Lord, make haste to help me."
>
> Rightly has this verse been selected from the whole Bible to serve this purpose. It suits every mood and temper of human nature, every temptation, every circumstance. It contains an invocation of God, a humble confession of

faith, a reverent watchfulness, a meditation on
human frailty, an act of confidence in God's
response, an assurance of his ever-present
support. The one who continuously invokes
God as his protector is aware that God is ever
at hand.

I repeat: each one of us, whatever one's
condition in the spiritual life, needs to use this
verse.

Perhaps wandering thoughts surge about
my soul like boiling water and I cannot control
them. I cannot offer prayer without it being
interrupted by silly images. I feel so dry that I
am incapable of spiritual feelings. Many sighs
and groans save me from dreariness. I must
needs say: "O God, come to my assistance. O
Lord, make haste to help me."

The mind should go on grasping this word
until it can cast away the abundance and
multiplicity of other thoughts and restrict itself
to the poverty of a single word. And thus it will
attain with ease that Gospel beatitude which
states: "Blessed are the poor in spirit for theirs
is the kingdom of heaven." Thus by God's light
the mind mounts to the manifold knowledge of
God and thereafter feeds on mysteries loftier
and more sacred.

John received from the lectio of a Spiritual Father a
word of life, as well as a deep and beautiful sharing
on the part of a Father who had already experienced
the rich potential of this word in his own life.

It was not only the Fathers and Mothers of the Desert who gave witness and proclaimed the fruitfulness of the Word, the nourishment that is to be found there. Let me conclude this chapter with a few words from one of the greatest theologians of that same period and all the succeeding periods of Church history, the great African bishop, Augustine of Hippo:

> "I will feed them on the heights of Israel." He has set up the authors of the divine Scriptures as the heights of Israel. Feed there to feed safely. Whatever you hear from that source, savor it well. Whatever is outside, reject. Lest you should go astray in the mist, listen to the shepherd's voice. Gather together on the mountain of holy Scripture. There are your heart's delights, there is nothing poisonous there, nothing you should not eat. Its pastures are the richest.

Chapter Six

Lectio in Context

Lectio—we see now that it is a word that has a deep and rich meaning, acquired over centuries of profound Christian experience. But more: whenever we say the word "lectio," we actually imply a whole process or way of spirituality—a journey into God, deep into the inner life of the Trinity.

Let's have a little Latin lesson, for the problem of translation still continues.

When we say "lectio," we always imply the whole process of *lectio–meditatio–oratio–contemplatio.* All four words can be translated by simply adding an "n" to them: lection–meditation–oration–contemplation. But in each case there is a problem in such a translation. Certainly much of the richness of the traditional meaning is lost.

Through the earliest days of the Church, distinc-
tions with regard to lectio were not readily made,
certainly not insisted upon. As we have seen, Abba
Isaac gave John Cassian a "word for contemplation." Receiving a word of life, which is the essence
of this particular kind of encounter with the Lord,
was for the venerated Father nothing less than to
enter upon a way to contemplation.

As the transition was taking place, in the middle
of the twelfth century, from the patristic to the scholastic era, the ninth Prior of the Grand Chartreuse
produced a remarkable little treatise for his brother. In
his *Ladder of Monks,* Guigo II clearly distinguishes
these four steps, or degrees, as he calls them. Yet he
insists on their inner relation and codependence:

> The first degrees are of little or no use without
> the last, while the last can never, or hardly ever,
> be won without the first. . . . Lectio without
> meditatio is sterile, meditatio without lectio is
> liable to error, oratio without meditatio is
> lukewarm, meditatio without oratio is unfruitful,
> oratio when it is fervent wins contemplatio, but
> to obtain it without oratio would be rare, even
> miraculous.

We certainly need all four elements. For the
monastics, who have the wonderful gift of holy
leisure, the four are usually experienced as an
organic whole. They simply sit down with their text,
in hand or in memory, and meet the Lord there in

his Word. How much time they spend on a particular occasion receiving the Word or letting it re-echo in their minds and hearts before they begin to respond can certainly vary. Indeed, it is in a sense a very natural interaction, this receiving and giving, as they sit with their Friend. At which precise moment they lapse into the deep rest of contemplation depends much on his presence and grace. Benedict's *Rule for Monasteries*, besides providing for a good bit of community reading, provides simply for periods of lectio, spaces for the whole process to be enjoyed.

As much as the four elements belong together and are part of a vital relationship, yet given the hectic world that most live in and the lack of that leisurely space at least on a regular basis, it is good to look at each of the elements individually and to take care to provide space for them in one's life.

∼ *Lectio* ∼

This first element refers to the gathering of the Sacred Text and the plucking of the Word that we will use all day to remember God's message to us.

∼ *Meditatio* ∼

Meditation is certainly a word that has different meanings. If you ask traditional Catholics about

meditation they will probably tell you about one of
the methods developed by the various saints after
the Protestant Reformation: the method of St.
Alphonsus or St. Sulpice, and so on. In these methods, it is a question of taking a scene or a thought
from the Scriptures and applying the mind and
imagination and memory to it, seeking all the while
to break through and come to the experience of the
Reality that is behind it. At least that should be the
intent. There is the danger of getting caught up in
one's own thoughts and ideas, images and insights—
a danger that is not absent from lectio. Since the
false self is made up of what I have and what I do, it
makes a play here to do something, to create some
brilliant ideas and insights and then to hang on to
them. All our thoughts, ideas, and insights, all our
creations are in danger of becoming idols. We have
to be ready to break them to pieces and pass beyond
them to the Reality that they of their nature point to.

If the traditional Catholic would usually understand
meditation in the sense of an active discursive
process, I think very many if not most today think
more readily of a more contemplative process when
they hear of meditation. Transcendental Meditation,
Zen meditation, and yoga have done much to form
the modern understanding of the word. People think
of meditation as some kind of process or discipline
they can practice to achieve if not absolute transcen-
dence at least some deep quieting of the mind and
body and a release of stress.

While Guigo's understanding of meditation comes
close to the first, neither of these responds to the
understanding and practice of the first millennium of
Christian life. In that earlier period, meditation
meant that, having received a word of life from one's
lectio or from a spiritual Father or Mother, we
carried that word with us, repeating it, perhaps even
on the lips but certainly in the mind, until it formed
the heart and called forth the response of prayer.
The Fathers spoke of the mind descending into the
heart. The word was to be received not only men-
tally but also affectively, expanding the listening that
we are, opening us to allow the fullness of Reality to
come in, to see things as God sees them, forming in
us the mind of Christ. Meditation was not so much
an active process whereby we worked with what we
had received until it fitted into the conceptual frame-
work we already had—rather, it was a more receptive process allowing the Word to break open and
reform us. It is not a wholly passive process; a
certain assimilation on our part is necessary. The
Fathers, inspired by the biblical admonition, "Taste
and see how good the Lord is," liked to use the
image of cattle and other biblically "clean" animals
who chew the cud. After gathering through lectio,
perhaps in the coolness of the morning, through the
day we chew upon what we have received, allowing
it to be assimilated through the processes of the day.

How different would our day be if we took from
our lectio a word like, "Whatever you do to the least,

you do to me," and it kept sounding in our hearts all through the day? As we encounter each person, we hear again, "Whatever you do to the least you do to me"? It is the Christ—no matter what guise he comes in.

All the world remembers with reverence the little nun from Albania. Sitting with Mother Teresa and looking into her deep, deep brown eyes was a transforming experience. For she saw the Christ in you and reflected this back to you, and you had a new sense of yourself. I have many memories of my time with Mother, but one stands out for me.

It was the practice in the novitiate in Calcutta for the second-year novices to go out in the morning with the ambulances to the train station to pick up the abandoned dying who were left there during the night. Mother, when she was home, usually went with them. On this particular day, among those they returned with was a man in a most sad condition. Rats had gnawed at him, maggots had eaten to the bone, he had not long to live. Mother herself claimed the privilege of caring for him. For much of an hour she did all she could to make him comfortable. As she was gently cooling his face, he opened his eyes, said "Thank you," and died. Mother rose, went to his feet, and prostrated herself full length. Later that day she told me, with a radiant smile, "I had the privilege this morning of caring for the dying Christ."

The Word, coming to live in us through meditation, transforms our listening. Yes, we see Christ in

the least, in everyone. And we know the joy of
loving and serving him in each.

∼ *Oratio* ∼

Almost naturally, this ongoing meditation calls forth
again and again a response: thanksgiving, praise,
petition, repentance, adoration. How present is God
in all and acting through all. The world is shot
through and through with the mercy and love of God.
Each one is the Christ. We come to constant prayer,
to praying without ceasing, praying in all we do.

I almost wish I could take the word "prayer" and
throw it out and begin over with some new word.
We all have so much baggage around that word.
Whenever I hear it, one of the images that comes to
my mind is little Sister Floretta, who taught me in
the second grade. I can still experience Sister standing over me, saying in no uncertain terms: "When
you pray, kneel up straight, fold your hands, close
your eyes. . . . " Even as a second-grader, I thought:
This is a funny way to talk to my Father.

Prayer is any and every kind of communication
with our God who loves us. If our listening is for
God, our whole life is prayer. Meditation is grounded
on lectio, which is a listening for God in his Word
and in his creation. And meditation, the abiding
presence of the Word on our lips and in our hearts,
in its turn helps to form and expand such listening.

Practically speaking, if each day we can do some lectio early in the day—perhaps we could use a bed Bible—and choose a word of life, we can begin to carry it with us through the day. At first we might need to use some reminders, for example, forming the deliberate intent to repeat our word each time we hear a clock strike, each time we pass through a door, when we walk down a corridor or street. Some effort, some schooling, will quickly make the practice ours. We will find our word returning more and more, coloring the way we see and think and act, making the Lord present so that we communicate with him, maybe in thought, maybe in word, maybe just in a sense of presence, of "withness."

Life is a very different experience when this kind of meditation has taken hold of us. There is something of a deep joy in knowing that a loving friend is with us in all. There is a benignity towards all, a joy in serving and in giving joy to others. There is a sense of peace and security: our present Friend is the God who has the whole wide world in his hand. We have nothing to fear. A simple practice: just repeating a word, carrying a word with us. But it can be so transforming.

~ *Contemplatio* ~

There is something wonderful about a deep love, the love after the uncontrolled passion is spent. It is the love of just *being with.* This is contemplation.

I have often said that I first learned contemplation the summer I was four years old. That summer I was on the farm with my grandparents. For some reason it was just the three of us at times. After supper I would go out on the porch and sit on the top step. After a bit, Granddad would come out and sit on one end of the porch swing. After a while, Grandma would come (women always do more work than men). And we would usually just sit there in silence. I felt so wonderful! It was only years later that I realized what was happening. This man and woman, who had been together for so many decades, had no need to say anything. It had all been said. They just sat together in love. And that love embraced the little grandson on the top step. He felt good all over as he sat in that love. Now he sits in the love of his heavenly Father.

Contemplation. Etymology is often instructive: *"tion"* bespeaks an abiding state; *"con"* means "with"—communion, union with; the *"templa"* was the segment of the heavens that the pagan priests of ancient Rome used to watch; by observing the flight of birds through the *templa*, they came to know the will of the gods. In time the *templa* became the *templum*—the temple—the place one went to know the will of the gods and to worship them. What is the temple of the new covenant? We are the temple of the new covenant, the covenant in his Blood, which we celebrate and receive in the Eucharist. *Contemplation:* to abide with God within his temple.

The whole process, if we have the space for it, can be present in each or any period of lectio. As we listen to the Word *(lectio),* a word, a phrase, a sentence may well strike us, and we let it reverberate within, opening and expanding, forming and shaping *(meditatio),* calling forth varied responses *(oratio)* until finally we simply rest in the Reality to which it all leads *(contemplatio).*

But any particular meeting with the Lord in lectio might not be so abundantly blessed, and we will, after listening, have to choose a word to take with us, allowing this word to be present to us as we go on about our daily responsibilities *(meditatio).* This word will, by God's presence and grace, again and again in the course of the day, illumine what we are encountering and call forth a response to the Divine Presence *(oratio).* And there will also be times when we will let everything else go and just sit quietly in Centering Prayer *(contemplatio).* Thus the process is spread out over the course of the day.

~ *Centering Prayer* ~

Even within the practice of Centering Prayer the fourfold process unfolds. Our time of Centering begins with a movement of faith, called forth by words arising from our memory (lectio): "I am with you at all times." "The Kingdom of God is within." "The Father and I will come and make our home in you." "Be still and know that I am God." We let the word of faith be present to us *(meditatio)* and respond with a movement of love *(oratio)* that comes to rest at the center *(contemplatio)*.

Thus in different ways the weave of listening, hearing, responding, and resting becomes the very fabric of our life lived in relation with God.

I have found that confusion sometimes arises among those who are following this simple traditional way of Christian prayer because I have used the expression "word" in the packaging for both lectio and Centering Prayer (see Appendices Two and Three). Perhaps it would have been wiser to avoid this. In the method for lectio, for example, I could have said "Take a morsel," or something like that. But the use of "word" is very traditional. As I have explained, a seeker would go to a spiritual father or mother and ask for a "word of life." In this context "word" can and usually does mean a phrase or sentence—and not just literally a word. Today we cannot so readily approach a spiritual father or mother; we can, however, readily ourselves approach the Sacred Text to receive a "word" under the guidance of Holy Spirit. So in formulating the simple method of lectio, I have kept the traditional expression, using "word" with the understanding that it is a word, a phrase, or a sentence received from the Scriptures under the guidance of Holy Spirit.

However, in the new packaging of the Prayer of the Heart or Centering Prayer, when I use the expression "word," I mean it quite literally. Here, too, I am following tradition. The author of *The Cloud of Unknowing* said to his spiritual son: "Choose a word, a simple word—a single-syllable word like 'God' or 'love' is best—but choose a word that is meaningful to you." So in Centering Prayer we use a single, simple word, a word we have chosen. And we usually use this same word every time we center. It is a word to which we have attached a certain meaning—it is meaningful to us— and that meaning is ultimately: "Lord, I am all yours. I give myself to you in love." Or as Father Thomas Keating more philosophically expresses it: "It is a symbol of our intention to consent to God's presence and action in us."

While the "word" we use in Centering Prayer usually remains the same for us day in and day out, year in and year out, the "word" we receive or take from our lectio usually differs each time we enjoy lectio. It is a word for the day, and it is carried through the day until our next period of lectio, shedding its particular light on the experiences we have with the Lord as we walk through that day. It is a word that gives meaning to many other things and brings new meaning into our lives. It is a very active word, inviting us to use our minds to the full to explore and discover—far different from the "word" of Centering Prayer, which invites us to rest quietly within at the center of our being by leaving behind all thoughts.

We seek God in love with our whole mind, heart, soul, and strength. The word of lectio helps us to do this at the conceptual and affective level; the word of Centering Prayer helps us to do this at the transcendent level, the level of being. We need both in our lives.

As Abba Isaac drew out so beautifully for John Cassian, as Guido so clearly affirmed, lectio is complete only in contemplation. It comes to contemplation and to life with a contemplative dimension by way of meditation and prayer. This is the simple, connatural way of spiritual life and growth as it was understood by the early Church, the Church of the first millennium. And it seems wholly apt for the Church and the Christians of the third millennium.

Chapter Seven

The Way of Friendship

This question is often raised at workshops and retreats: "What should I read at my lectio? How do I know what text to use?"

As St. Paul told St. Timothy: "All Scripture inspired by God is useful for teaching and refutation, for correction and putting us in the way that is right with God, for communication and communion." For our lectio we can use any text of Scripture we want. Some like to open the Bible at random to see what the Lord has to say to them today. This is fine, though we should avoid all superstitious attitudes, looking for the Lord to give us through the Bible infallible answers to particular questions. That is not usually his way. He has given us a mind to use and the constant help of Holy Spirit.

Many prefer to use the readings of the day for their daily lectio. This is very good. Listening with the Church, there is special grace present. Apt passages from the Hebrew Bible and the apostolic writings are given us as a rich setting for hearing the Gospels. When these texts are used at our lectio we can then easily share with others in the Church who are doing the same. However, restricting ourselves to these does have the disadvantage that some passages of Scripture will never be read, for they are not among the passages used in the liturgy.

Others like to follow the *lectio continuata*, which has been the common practice in monasteries. Certain books of the Bibles are assigned to particular seasons of the year: Isaiah for Advent, Jeremiah for Lent, Lamentations for Holy Week, the Epistles of John for the Easter time, and so on. During the assigned season, the book is read through, chapter by chapter.

Most find their preferred lectio in the Gospels, and so some will read these through. The Gospels certainly are a good place for beginners to start.

Some of us have favorite passages in Scripture and like to return to them. But we soon enough find, sometimes to our surprise, that these much-loved passages can be used by the Lord to bring us very different messages on different days. For the Lord always speaks to us right where we are today. This is one of the things that makes lectio such a rewarding experience. It is always relevant, and therefore it is always new. It is a living Word speaking to us in the onrush of life.

We can also choose texts from men and women of faith, friends of God. As long as they are "faith-full" in their writings, theirs are writings drawn from and reflecting the Word of God. Indeed, the writings of those special friends of God, whom we call the Fathers of the Church, are often so full of the inspired Word that they are veritable mosaics of Scripture. They leave us with the strong impression that these writers knew the Bible by heart, indeed, carried it in their heart.

However, I personally think that for the most part we do best turning to the inspired Word itself for our lectio and using the other texts more for study and motivational reading. Among my favorite texts are the words that came so directly from the heart of Jesus as he spoke to his chosen twelve at the Last Supper. He tells us then: "I no longer call you servants, but friends, because I make known to you all that I have received from the Father. . . . You have not chosen me, no, I have chosen you." Wondrous, indeed, it is: to be the chosen friend of God himself!

Let us take a little look at this tremendously beautiful reality called friendship.

How does it begin?

Well, first we get acquainted. Perhaps we go to a party. As we enter, the hostess comes over to greet

us and guides us across the room to meet another
guest: "Maria, this is Robert. Robert, this is Maria. I
know you are both interested in scuba diving." Then
our charming hostess glides off to welcome someone else, leaving us standing there facing one another. "What did you say your name is?" We take up
the conversation. "Where are you from?" "Are you
really interested in scuba diving?" If the evening goes
well, there is a good chance that before it ends
Robert will say to Maria: "What are you doing
Saturday? Would you like to go scuba diving?"
Robert and Maria will have become acquainted.

Well, they do go scuba diving on Saturday, and
soon they are doing other things together. As they
do, they begin to know each other better, more now
through the way they act and the things they share
than just their words. They get to know each other's
like and dislikes, what they value, and where they
agree. They get to be quite friendly.

If this goes on for some time, they may come to
be real friends. A friend is someone who is there for
you, one you can count on. If you are going away
for the weekend, you call on your friend to take care
of the dog. If you run out of gas, you call your
friend. If you need a shoulder to cry on or want to
share a deep personal joy, you turn to your friend.
Your friend won't let you down.

As a friendship matures, it can give birth to a
deep sense of oneness. There is a joy in being
together, a good sense of being. And it might well

happen that Robert and Maria will walk down the aisle and make their vows so that they can be together until death does them part.

From *acquaintanceship* a *friendly* relationship can grow to produce true *friends,* who can come to know a deep oneness or *union* in spirit.

The traditional Christian way of lectio takes our Lord's words seriously. It is a response to his overtures, his choice. It is a way of friendship.

We get acquainted with God through his Word. Of course, he knows all about us, but *we* need to get to know *him*. And getting acquainted is not a once-and-for-all thing. Very many marriages fail, sometimes after years of married life, because the man is still in love with the woman he went on the honeymoon with and does not know the magnificent woman who has matured at his side. And vice versa. There is a wonderful movement called Marriage Encounter. After an initial, vitalizing, long weekend, the participants are sent forth with a commitment to "ten and ten." The partners commit themselves to spend ten minutes each day writing to each other revealing just where they are in their life's journey and in their relationship with each other. Then they exchange the letters. After they have had time to read them and reflect, they spend at least ten minutes talking frankly about what they have written. The Lord has sent us wonderful love letters in the Scriptures. Our lectio is part of our "ten and ten," enabling us each day to become more fully acquainted with him, and in that relationship getting more fully acquainted with ourselves.

As we carry the word we have received at lectio with us, the Lord walks with us, commenting through that word on the things we experience through the day. It enables us to begin to see things more the way he sees them as well as to experience that he is there with us, helping us and supporting us in all.

Let me share just one experience with you. I usually do my lectio early in the morning. On this particular day, the Lord just didn't seem to show up. I had turned to my favorite section, the Last Supper discourse, but nothing really opened for me. So at the end of my time I had to choose a word to carry with me. I chose our Lord's words: "I am the Way."

A few hours later, I was walking down from the monastery to the guesthouse. As I walked along, my word was with me. Suddenly I realized that I was not just walking down a road. I was walking *in the way.* That all the walking I do, whether in the cloister, or out on the road, or in the streets of the city, or along corridors—it is all in the way. It is in the Lord and with the Lord and on the way to life eternal. Since that morning all my walking has been different; it has been in the way. Through his Word, my Friend enabled me to see things more his way.

When I arrived at the guesthouse, there was a young man waiting for me. He had all the problems in the book and a few that weren't. As I sat there listening to him, I was asking the Lord: "What do I say to this poor dear lad." Then the Lord sort of poked me in the ribs. Oh, yes! And I told the young man about my Friend, who is the Way. As I shared this word with this fellow, it was as if great burdens were falling off his shoulders. Now he had a way to go. The Lord had given me that word that day not only for myself but also for this other friend of his.

Later that day, around 4:45, I was climbing up the steps to the church. There are more steps between the guesthouse and the church than I have ever had the courage to count. I was exhausted. It had been a very full day. And I was saying to the Lord: "Lord, how will I ever get through Vespers? I will sing every note flat." And once again he kind of gave me a little poke. "Oh, yes! *You* are the way." And I went on to sing Vespers with my Friend with a lot of energy and joy.

Our Friend is someone we can really count on. St. James tells us in his epistle that the reason our prayer is not heard is because we are like the waves of the sea: up and down, up and down. I believe, I don't believe. I trust, I don't trust. Our Lord has told us that if we tell yonder mountain to move and do not waver in our hearts, it will move. But we waver all over the place. Through lectio and meditatio we come to know what a friend we have in Jesus. We arrive at the place where we can truly pray.

And then there are those times when enough is said. We don't need any more words. We just want to be there with the Lord. We hear his pressing invitation: *"Come to me, you who work hard and are overburdened. I will refresh you."* And we sit quietly there, content with the poverty of a single simple word that says it all.

Lectio	Acquaintanceship
Meditatio	Friendly companionship
Oratio	Friendship
Contemplatio	Union

It is the way of Christian friendship.

"I call you friends because I make known to you all that the Father has made known to me."

"Listen to my voice," the Lord said through the prophet Jeremiah, *"then I will be your God and you will be my people."*

"Hear, O Israel."

God is not truly God for us if we do not listen to him. If God is who God is—the source of all, the all-wise, the one who knows, who knows us and the meaning of our being and our lives because he made us—if we know this, we listen to him. We acknowledge all this by listening. If we do not listen, we virtually deny that he is God, at least in relation to our lives. This is just the fundamental relationship between Creator and creature. By its very self, our listening postulates lectio. But we have been called to so much more. Not just creatures called to listen to a Creator who has every right to demand anything and everything of us. Not just servants: "I no longer call you servants." But friends. What are the rights that a friend has to demand that we listen? And what kind of a listening can he or she rightly expect?

We dare to come to lectio as friends with heartfelt longing truly to hear our Friend, truly to understand, that we might understand him and be more and more one with him. We come to lectio with a great longing for union, the union we call contemplation. (That word, too, might well be retired to give place to a word not so loaded with baggage.) Our lectio postulates a very special kind of listening, a listening that gives tremendous meaning to our lives. It is a listening that is filled with faith and trust, hope and love. It is the kind of listening that makes lectio one of the most wonderful things in our lives. In this listening, our lectio is a time that comes to be filled with what is the greatest joy of human life, a time of being with—being with our most intimate Friend.

For the wonderful gift of lectio, can we ever thank you enough, O Lord? For here you show us that indeed you are our Friend, for here you make known to us all that the Father has made known to you, all the deepest meaning of our lives, all the secrets of your own life in the Trinity, all that we are called to, all to which we aspire, all the longings of our heart.

Chapter Eight

He Is Never Alone

God and me.

Some people are suspicious not only of the contemplative life but of any talk about contemplative union or intimacy with God. They feel there is necessarily something self-centered or narcissistic about it. God and me—and to hell with the rest of you!

They are right, in a way. Those pursuing a more intimate union with God do have to be a bit suspicious of their own motivation. I can remember my first spiritual Father saying to me with some vehemence: "Seek the God of consolations, not the consolations of God." We can pursue lectio or contemplation because we like the good feelings we get, whether these flow from feeling good about ourselves or because we have fashioned a God who is cuddly and warm, a God who cuddles us.

Lectio in itself can become a very satisfying mental and emotional experience. We can feel we are getting wonderful ideas and inspirations, insights well worth jotting down. Unfortunately, it is true that a very self-satisfying practice can masquerade as true lectio.

There are warning signs that this might be the case. One of them might be the unwillingness to move on to contemplation and leave behind all our beautiful insights. Our beautifully fashioned ideas can become our idols, all the more deceptive because they are so beautiful and drawn from the divinely inspired Word itself.

A more certain sign is what is going on in our lives. Our Lord has told us that we can judge a tree by its fruit. What is the fruit of our spiritual practice? If we are becoming more selfish, more jealous of our time and routine, more elated by our spiritual progress, less caring about others, and less concerned about their well-being, then we do indeed need to question our spiritual practices.

But if one is practicing true lectio, then those who are concerned about narcissism need have no fears.

∼ *Divine Friendship* ∼

It is only by God's grace that one begins to take lectio seriously. And only by God's grace does one

persevere in it. Anyone who has resolved to meet
the Lord daily in lectio knows how challenging it is
to keep such a resolution. In fact, resolutions don't
usually work. There has to be a deeper commitment
than that. We have to take a stand and make a
declaration: I am a person who meets the Lord each
day as a friend and disciple, sitting at his feet to
receive a word of life. When we define ourselves in
this way, then even if we miss sometimes, we will
return to our practice, because this is who we are.
All of this is the working of God's grace in us.

Even given this commitment, the challenges will
be many. Life does tend to get so full. The simple
asceticism of carving out time for the Lord is demanding. More demanding still is to come to our
lectio with the proper attitude, so that it can be true
lectio. We have to let go of all our doings for a bit.
We have to let go of our prejudices and precon-
ceived ideas. We have to be an openness, a stillness
that can receive the Word and allow it to come alive
in us, bringing whatever message, whatever challenge it wants to bring to us at the moment. True
lectio calls for the courage to face the Friend squarely
and let all our shoddiness and infidelity and selfishness be exposed. Yes, sometimes our experience of
God in lectio can be tremendously consoling. But
other times, and these might well be more frequent,
our lectio can be a very painful encounter with Truth.

It doesn't stop there. This Divine Friend, whom
we meet in lectio, is a Man and a God of infinite

self-giving love. Just to be with him challenges. And
certainly it humbles, when we realize his goodness to
us and our poor return. But he does not hesitate to
go on and make demands of us that will stretch us to
the utmost. He has given himself in love for every
man, woman, and child on this planet. Calling us to
intimate friendship, he will not be content until we
join him in this mission of salvation. He wants us to
be with him in this. Just how that is to be accomplished is something that will unfold, that will be
discerned with time. He is a most caring and gentle
Friend. He will lead us step by step, ever with us.

Yes, ever with us. But here is another aspect of
this demanding friendship. He has a way of being
with us that sometimes is experienced as a terrible
absence. It is at such times that he seems to say most
insistently, "Go and bring the love and concern you
have for me to me in your needy sister and brother."

The Friend we meet in lectio is never alone. (That
doesn't leave much room for a God-and-me huddle.)
He is the head of a body. He is the master who
summons disciples only to send them out. And he
doesn't send them out well supplied—at least in the
things of this world. He chooses the way of weak-
ness so that nothing may glory in his sight. God is
God—all the glory is his.

This Friend whom we meet in our lectio is the one
who has declared: "Mary has chosen the better part
and it shall not be taken away from her." This is the
one who defended that Mary when she "wasted"

thousands of dollars in a lavish show of love for him.
He is the one who says: "Come to me. I will refresh
you. Let us go apart for a while." He does want us
to waste ourselves on him, pouring out some of the
precious ointment of our lives upon him, enjoying
time apart with him.

And yet he is the Judge who tells us that when the
time for judging comes, we will be judged on what
we did for him in the needy, the hungry, the thirsty,
the sick, the imprisoned, the homeless. We cannot
afford to sit quietly with our Bible and think that is all
we have to do.

One of those wonderful stories from the desert
comes to my mind. A couple of curious pilgrims
arrived at the cell of a hermit who was reputed to be
very holy. The holy man welcomed them into his
humble abode and did what he could to make them
comfortable. As they looked about the sparsely
furnished room, they noted how little was there. Piles
of palm leaves would undoubtedly have to serve for
their beds. The floor was a good enough place to sit.
But what scandalized them was that this holy man did
not have even a Bible on his windowsill. After the
frugal repast he shared with them, one of them, with
not too much delicacy, questioned the old man about
this apparent lack. The reply was very simple: "The
book that told me I should sell what I have and give
to the poor I sold and gave the money to the poor."

There is not much value in our having the Book
enthroned in our home, or even in our hand, if we

do not take what it says into our heart. And that is precisely what those who do true lectio do. They take to heart the words of the Book. They feed the hungry Christ. They clothe the naked Christ. They give drink to the thirsty Christ. They visit the imprisoned Christ. They open their door to the homeless Christ. They comfort the sick Christ.

Obviously, we cannot all do all these things. But none of us can sit comfortably at our lectio day by day if we are not responding to the Christ in the ways he presents himself to us in his need. It is too much of a contradiction. Our Friend will not let us get away with it.

True, we do have an immense power for self-deception, for rationalization. But the peace that only the Lord can give will not come into our hearts. Nor the graces we need to be consistently kind, joyful, loving, and long-suffering. The absence of these fruits of the Spirit in our lives will soon enough undermine our self-deception.

∼ A Companion on the Way ∼

Still, it is good to have someone walking with us on the way. It doesn't necessarily have to be a priest or a religious or someone who has a degree in spiritual counseling. I honestly fear those who take up the label of spiritual director. They might try to actually direct people! But we can all be helped by a friend

who loves us, enters into our aspirations, and is
ready to help us pursue them. A friend who will pray
with us and help us listen to what the Spirit is saying
to us. A friend who will be there to help us along
when we need help, to affirm us when we are
courageously living our complete "yes" to the Lord,
and to give us a good, swift kick in the pants when
we are lagging behind. Someone who will be willing
to tell us when we are kidding ourselves. A good clue
that we are deceiving ourselves in something is when
we are reluctant to speak openly to our friend about
it, when we find ourselves coloring the story as we
share it. Of course, if such a friend is knowledgeable
in the things of the spiritual journey and, even better,
is more experienced in them, that is all to the good.

Such a friendship is truly precious. Anyone who is
serious about the spiritual journey will seek out such
a person. It is not an imposition to ask someone to
walk with us in this way. It is a grace for them. The
Lord will give them the graces they need to respond
to our faith-filled expectation, graces they otherwise
would not receive. They will necessarily be challenged
by the friendship to be more faithful themselves. And,
of course, we will bring to this friend a special love
that will express itself in our prayer for our friend.

Of the many stories of how the Lord has called
forth men and women through lectio, let me recall
some of the classics. We have already mentioned
Anthony, the Father of monasticism. It was when he
heard the word "Go, sell what you have . . . "—heard

the word not once but twice—that he went forth to
the desert and started that great procession of saints.
It was not long after that event that Augustine heard:
"Take and read." And the word he received brought
about his conversion and gave the Church one of its
great Fathers. Lectio was almost forced upon
Ignatius of Loyola. He resisted it. But in time it again
brought about a conversion that gave the Church
another great blessing, the Society of Jesus.

The Martha–Mary tension should live in all of us
because it lives in the teaching of Christ. It is a good
tension because it challenges us constantly to exam-
ine our lives and our fidelity to the Word. We want
to ask ourselves continually: "Am I doing enough?
Am I as faithful as I can be to my Friend's call to
intimacy? Am I doing all I can for him in his need?
Am I keeping my life sourced in him so that I can do
ever more? Am I the source of spiritual energy for
the Church that I should be?" This is the language of
a lover. And this is the language of one who daily
meets the Lord in true lectio.

If I am not driven by such questions—not necessarily in a feverish, exaggerated way, but in a way that
speaks to my heart and brings a certain anguish to my
prayer—then maybe I do need to question the listening I bring to lectio. If I am content to gather beautiful
thoughts in a book and feel good about myself because I am so faithful to my lectio, then maybe I had
better get rid of my book, stop collecting thoughts,
and let some of the Lord's words sear my soul.

Paul has a frightening and challenging statement: we are to "fill up what is wanting in the passion of Christ." It is words like these encountered in our lectio that certainly keep any true practice of lectio from ever becoming a God-and-me huddle. Lectio brings us to a deeper understanding of the God who sent his Son to die for us. We come to understand a bit more the heart of the Prodigal Father. We come to understand a bit more the mystery of the cross and how this loving Father can ask his Son—and us whom he has come to love as his Son—to give himself in love. As we meet him each day and let him speak to our hearts, we come to know something more of the mystery of Divine Love. And we find a joy and a peace in patience and long-suffering. We begin to understand what the Lord is saying when he tells us that the first and the greatest commandment is to love the Lord our God with our whole mind and our whole heart and our whole soul. And what it means when he immediately adds: "The second is like unto this, love your neighbor as yourself." We cannot possibly love God with our whole being if we do not love what he loves and how he loves. Christ loves us as his very own body. And we are indeed one in his body. The true self is the self we all are in Christ and in his love.

∼ *An Image of Lectio* ∼

Recently someone gave me a mandala. Around the outside of the circular design were six words. The first four we are familiar enough with: the traditional *lectio, meditatio, oratio, contemplatio.* To these were added two others: *compassio* and *operatio.* They do indeed complete the sequence. Within the mandala were short definitions of each of the six:

LECTIO

Reading is a gentle opening of one's whole being to the Saving Word of God. We allow the Word to nourish us as the words are read not for information but rather for transformation.

MEDITATIO

Meditation is the simple repetition of words or phrases that capture our attention. It is not an intellectual exercise, thinking about the text, but a surrender, through the repetition, to allow the Word to penetrate more deeply into our being until we become one with the text.

ORATIO

Prayer is the response of the heart to God. Filled with the Saving Word, we make our response. As St. Cyprian says, "In Scripture, God speaks to us, and in prayer we speak to God."

CONTEMPLATIO

Contemplation. As we are faithful to the dynamic of lectio there are those moments when we find ourselves just present to the One who is eternally present to us. This contemplative awareness is a pure gift of God. It is not a product of our work or a reward for it.

COMPASSIO

Compassion is one of the fruits of prayer and contemplation. In this encounter with God our whole being is opened up to experience the brokenness of all creation. We find ourselves united not only with God but with all who live.

OPERATIO

Action. Things are already different by our engagement in lectio, but we may find ourselves called to engage in other actions that will help others. God invites us to act and then empowers us, directing our steps in the way of peace.

With perhaps one reservation, I like this presentation very much. I find the identification of contemplation with what is called infused contemplation unfortunate. The author seems to imply that it is a relatively rare thing, and that one just has to wait until it comes. This presentation contains shades of the idea that used to be quite prevalent: contemplation was only for very special people like enclosed nuns. The rest of us had to keep at it with active forms of prayer and maybe, just maybe, before we died, we might be gifted with this experience of God. In fact, I think what some authors have called acquired contemplation (I am not too happy with the terminology) is quite common. A decision to rest in the Lord with a simple word of love is something that anyone who loves the Lord receives the grace to do in response to the Lord's invitation: "Come to me, and I will refresh you." Grace is, of course, present and necessary for all forms of prayer. But with God's grace so lavishly given, anyone can rest in his love. And this alone is a form of contemplation.

All those who regularly meet the Lord in lectio will go beyond all the thoughts and ideas and concepts, no matter how fascinating they are, and enter into a contemplative union with God in Christ. They will come to have the mind and heart of Christ, which is a heart of self-giving love, ever ready to give itself totally for the salvation and well-being of the human family.

Chapter Nine

Some Days . . .

Some days we come to our lectio and it seems as though the Lord forgot it was our lectio time. He just doesn't show up! Words, words, and more words. We have heard them all before. They are not freighted with meaning. They are just words.

When I was a young boy living in Freeport, a wonderful little brook ran through the woods near our home. For me, the brook became a fascinating friend. I spent many hours near it and in it. The shallow water went rushing along, running over rocks and stones in some places. Through the years it had polished them to a perfect smoothness, bringing out all the wonderful tracing and color within them. Sometimes I would lie naked in the cool, clear water, letting it run the full length of my body. I felt as if it were making *me* smooth and clean and clear.

Now, when one of those days arrive and it is just words, words, and more words, I think of that very wonderful little brook. Some people speak of "dark nights," others of dryness. But the Word of God is never really dark or dry. It is lustrous water, flowing over me. It may seem to be just words for me today, but as the Word of the Lord washes over my mind and heart, I feel it cleaning, cleansing deeply, smoothing, calling forth the beauty. People often comment on the light, the joy, the "something" they see in my eyes. I think it is just the Lord letting them see something of what he is working in me. Lectio, especially in its full experience of *contemplatio*, cleans us, smooths things out—it's that sense of peace that comes—and allows something of the beauty of the image of God that we are to shine forth.

Sitting with the Word of God, listening, whether the words are being brought to our inner ear by the voice of another or through our own eyes, is a time of communion, even when the Lord seems absent and the words seem to be just words.

~   *Aids to Understanding*   ~

But this doesn't preclude our making some efforts to make the Word more meaningful to us. Some have found that writing helps. They come to lectio with

pen and paper in hand, a notebook or a journal. As
thoughts and insights come, they might jot them
down, or perhaps, so as not to interfere with their
full attention to the Presence, they might wait until
the end of their lectio time to start writing. There is,
of course, a great danger in this practice. The false
self can quickly change our time of meeting with the
Lord into a search for bright and stimulating ideas to
write down. We have to take care that we keep first
things first. We go to lectio to be with the Lord. If
our lectio doesn't pass into *contemplatio*, we might
ask whether we are not getting too caught up with
the words and insights, the stimulation of the mind
and the filling of the chest of memory.

But when the Word does not seem to speak to us,
it can sometimes help to jot down a chosen word or
phrase and then to invite a certain amount of free
association, especially allowing other Scripture texts
to surface. They can throw oblique light on the day's
text and perhaps open up a whole chain of thought.
This seems to be very much part of the approach of
the Fathers. Aelred of Rievaulx comes to mind. As
he was preparing a Palm Sunday sermon, mention
of the unbinding of the colt that was to carry the
Lord led Aelred to think of a cord and then of the
sevenfold cord that was used to bind Samson. With
that thread, Aelred wove into this Palm Sunday
sermon the whole story of Samson and what it has
to teach us. On another occasion, a Christmas
sermon, the phrase used by the shepherds, "Let us

go over and see," brought to the abbot's mind the
shepherd Moses when he spied the burning bush
and said to himself, "Let us go over and see." With
that association Aelred went on to interweave and
contrast the experience of Moses and the experience
of the shepherds called to the Lord's manger, the
Jewish dispensation and the Christian.

Associations need not be solely scriptural, though
these can be especially powerful. The whole of the
interaction of God with the Chosen People was
meant to prepare their minds and hearts to receive
the Word. So the inspired record of these events
does prepare and open our minds to receive that
Word more fully and fruitfully. Associations with the
everyday things of our life, of what is affecting our
life right now, can not only open the Word for us but
can open channels for its wisdom and consolation to
flow into today's step on the journey. Jotting down
these associations, webbing them, like speaking the
Word when we do our lectio, engages more of our
whole being. It also assists the memory in registra-
tion, retention, and retrieval. Again, though, I do
want to repeat: We don't want to mistake the finger
for the moon. We are not interested in the finger
that points to the moon; we are interested in seeing
the moon itself. We are not interested in our own
ideas and insights; we are interested in that to which
they should all point: the living Word and his Presence in the intimacy of this sharing moment of lectio
and in our lives throughout the day.

Scriptural associations and the preparatory role of the Jewish testament are helpful because the more familiar we are with the Sacred Text as a whole, the more easily the Word can come to us in fullness. Sacred study of the Scriptures opens the way to many insights, to a fuller understanding of the Word.

Let me give you just one example. Scripture scholars, in studying that all-important Last Supper that Jesus celebrated with his disciples, have largely seen it in the context of a Passover meal—a meal full of ritual. It would seem that when Jesus took a cup and blessed it and gave it to his disciples, it was the Cup of Blessing, the fourth cup of the ritual meal. At the usual Passover meal, though, as this part of the ritual took place, each one held his or her own cup and at the end of the blessing all drank simultaneously, each from his or her own cup. But it seems clear from the Gospel that this was not the case at this very special meal. Rather, all were invited to drink from the one cup. A new, deeper union and communion in the Blood of the new covenant was being offered to the Twelve (or eleven). From sacred study, knowing this little bit about the Jewish ritual makes us aware of something very special in our Lord's invitation to "take and drink . . . " that we might otherwise miss.

∼ *Rich Translations* ∼

I have mentioned above how much a familiarity with the biblical languages can add to our time with the

Word, even if we have to use an interlinear text.
Hebrew is such a simple—I might say, earthy—
language, so full of imagery, that it seems to invite
us more readily into an experience of the Word.
Hearing the Word resound in our ear very much as
Jesus did in the synagogue at Nazareth or the
Temple at Jerusalem has a certain intimacy about it.
We listen with him. And we know that today this
prophecy is fulfilled in our hearing. For its part, the
powerful richness of the Greek words, some of
which seem to have been created by the inspired
writers to carry the infinitely rich burden of the
Revelation, can greatly stimulate our own entrance
into these concepts.

Today we are blessed with an abundance of
excellent translations, especially in English. Each
translator is using his or her gifts, developed usually
through years of painstaking study, to help us to
enter more fully into the Word. It can be useful to
have several biblical translations at hand when we
are studying. When some particular word or phrase
speaks to us, we can seek a fuller entrance into its
meaning by consulting the various translators' ways
of trying to bring forth the fullness of its meaning.
Or when some text seems to defy our effort to make
sense of it, we can turn to other translators for help.
If we are familiar with more than one contemporary
language, we can use translations in the different
languages we know to bring in many more enriching
associations.

Commentaries can also be helpful. Like the translators, these men and women have used their gifts and their years of study to offer us insight into the Sacred Text. Some books unite the Text and commentary, like Doubleday's Anchor Bible. Father Dahood's three volumes on the Psalms are excellent. Barcley's has long been a favorite, recommended by such powerful men of the Word as Fulton Sheen. Perhaps the most popular biblical commentary in the United States today—especially useful because of its conciseness—is *The New Jerome Biblical Commentary,* published by Prentice Hall.

∼ *Shared Lectio* ∼

Belonging to a biblical study group or Bible-sharing group can be immensely helpful.

Father Patrick Peyton of blessed memory used to say: "The family that prays together, stays together." No one would doubt that. But I would say: The family that does lectio together not only stays together but grows ever more one. I am sure that is true of any authentic family prayer, but it is so obviously true where a family each day sits together at the Lord's feet, listening to him and then sharing together how they can bring the received Word into their lives as individuals and as family.

Some time ago I visited an aunt and uncle living in retirement in Florida. Can you guess where they

have their Bible enthroned in their home? On the
kitchen table. When they come down for breakfast
in the morning, the first course is always the Psalms,
the second, a reading from the Gospels. Then, as
they munch their toast and drink their coffee, they
share what they hear the Lord saying to them that
morning. What a wonderful way to start the day. And
how meaningfully rich their breakfast time together
has become. No wonder they are a deeply intimate,
very contented and loving couple in their old age.

I once had supper at the home of a very wealthy
and large family. As the meal concluded, the young-
est, then about five, went to the sideboard and
brought over a large humidor. I thought to myself, Is
he going to offer me a cigar? But when I opened the
chest I found it was full of rosaries. The little man
carried it around the table and each person took a
rosary. We said the usual introductory prayers, the
Creed, Our Father, and three Hail Marys. Then
Mary, who was perhaps around ten then, an-
nounced the mystery of the day. That evening it was
the Annunciation. She went on to tell us what it
meant to her. When she finished, others added a
thought or two. We spent about fifteen minutes
sharing our thoughts, then we prayed the decade of
the beads. That was it. The family rosary had moved
along for this family to become much more a shared
lectio. Today that mother (father has gone off to
heaven) rests content, knowing that her nine sons
and daughters are strong in the practice of their faith

and raising their children in much the same way. Sad to say, not too many parents enjoy the same consolation. But if the faith is not a living reality in the home, if the parents are not truly disciples of Jesus and living out the belief that he has the words of eternal life, then there is little possibility that the faith will be a living reality in the homes of their children.

A Bible study group should of its own nature move into shared prayer and contemplation. We can certainly profit by using some of the scholarship that comes out of the sterile classrooms and research halls of academia, though with caution. Sometimes it is very difficult for the Spirit of God (if I may put it that way) to guide the study of those who do not see as a living Word the Sacred Text that they are studying. A purely rationalistic approach to the Sacred Scriptures will always go astray; it misses too much. But our own studies should be very much in the context of prayer, depending deeply on Holy Spirit as well as on scholarship. There are some excellent Scripture scholars, men and women of true faith and prayer. Some of them have come into prominence in our time, like Father Raymond Brown, who made the cover of the Easter edition of *Time* magazine. We had best turn to them.

A study group can give us a certain amount of guidance in our study. If it is blessed with a good facilitator, we can be enriched by the fruit of the facilitator's scholarship as well as the insights of our fellow participants. But whether it is a study group or simply a Bible-sharing group, one of the great benefits that comes from participating in such a group is the support it gives us in being faithful to our daily lectio, especially during those days when the Lord doesn't seem to be around. There is a certain accountability, there is witness, and there is grace as we pray for one another and care for one another.

A support group does not have to be specifically a Bible-sharing group. I have often told pastors that their parish will be a success only when every member of the parish is in a small group, caring for others and being cared for. The group may be the gang that comes in on Friday evening to vacuum the church or the Centering Prayer group that meets on Thursday after work. But each group can be encouraged to spend a few minutes with the Word of the Lord. Let them listen to next Sunday's readings and share some of their insights. It has been a great consolation to me to see how lay people respond to an opportunity to do this and truly enjoy it. It is a good idea, however, to watch that it does not go on too long. It is better for everyone to go home wanting more than for any to be exhausted.

Those times when it seems the Lord hasn't kept his "date" are most precious. You are probably familiar with that classic little story of the footsteps in the sand. A traveler on the journey looked back one day. She noticed that sometimes there were two sets of footsteps in the sand, hers and her Lord's, who was accompanying her on the journey. But other times there was only one set of footprints. And these were the times when things were most difficult in her life. So she complained to the Lord, "Where were you when I most needed you?" The Lord replied, "There is only one set of prints in those places because it was then that I carried you."

When the Lord seems absent and we are still faithful, then his grace is working most powerfully in our lives. The Lord hides himself only that we might seek him all the more. Listen to Solomon's Song of Songs—a continuous game of hide-and-go-seek. Blessed are they who hunger, . . . they shall be filled. He fills the hungry with good things. It is the love of desire that grows. And this life is meant for growth. So be content when the Lord doesn't seem to show up for your session of lectio. Know that he is near. Just keep going. Be faithful to your practice. In time the desert will bloom.

Chapter Ten

Making Sense of the Senses

We hear of some rather ridiculous things today that go under the name of "biblical scholarship," like the so-called Jesus group that cast votes, in diversely colored beads, to determine which sayings in the New Testament are authentically Words of the Lord. Such nonsense is enough to turn one away from modern rationalistic scriptural studies. A reason that is not informed by faith and aided by Holy Spirit can hardly hope to attain to any truly fruitful understanding of the Word.

Nonetheless, we are commanded by the Lord to love him with our whole mind. We need to bring to the Scriptures the fullness of the mental powers that the Lord has given us, ever pressing our edges. It is largely the labor of scriptural study to get at the full meaning of the literal sense. God called forth men to give utterance to his inspired Word and to commit it to writing. These writers were men of their time; they expressed themselves precisely *as* men of their time. Hence, to understand them, we need to know the mores of those times and the meaning of words in that context. In the last chapter there was an example of this in regard to the Cup of Blessing. Within the context, the simple change our Lord introduced was rich with meaning.

∽ *The Importance of Context* ∽

Words certainly are historically defined. When I was young and gay, that expression meant something quite different from what it would mean today to say that someone is young and gay. When readers of the twenty-third century are enjoying the literature of the twentieth, they had best be aware of this evolution in language or they might read some strange things into stories coming from the first half of the century.

The literary genre is also very important. The efforts of scholars of past centuries to interpret the myths of Genesis in a literal, historical sense has led to interpretations that, if we are charitable, make us smile benignly. Even the pope had to apologize recently for the inhumane activity some of his prede-cessors took in the defense of an unenlightened literal interpretation of the Sacred Text when faced with the facts being presented by science. We might wonder if the same kind of exaggerated literalism is not still at work sometimes, for instance, in the question of the ordination of women. Especially in this scientific age, when many of us are much too prone to read everything literally and in a highly critical way, it is important as we listen to Scripture to understand what literary form the inspired writer is using to convey the divine teaching. Is it history, and how was history understood in those days? Is it prose, or is it poetry using all that poetic license allows? Or is it myth, a wonderful popular tale that enshrines some basic truth? Everybody loves stories. We remember stories and enjoy recounting them. They are good teaching devices. So God tells us the story of Genesis and many others. I think the Jewish people must have always delighted to hear the prophet Elisha tell the great Aramaean general to go jump in the river—seven times! Jonah's big fish (Was it a whale? At least it was a whale of a story!) continues to delight us in Walt Disney's *Pinocchio.* God's son, Jesus, told stories. And he interpreted some of his stories to help us get a start in the art of interpretation. If it hadn't been the Divine Teller himself who told us that the birds of the air are the devils, some of us might raise an eyebrow at such an interpretation. And so the devil can appear as a snake. . . .

There are fewer and fewer people around who actually experienced that night. But most of us have heard about it. Orson Welles broadcast a very vivid description of what portended to be the end of the world. Many of his listeners failed to understand that it was but a fabrication, a story. They took it for a factual news story and panicked. The panic was widespread, and Welles was later roundly condemned. Many condemn God because his Scriptures are not the literal history that their listening is so narrowly geared to hear. It is important that we attune our hearing to the genre the Broadcaster is using.

There is another sense to be found in Scripture that *is* intended by the Lord, yet which goes beyond the literal, even when it is understood in its historical context and according to its literary genre. St. Paul points us to it, although Jesus himself had already done this when he spoke of the prophet Elijah and John the Baptizer. In writing to his Galatian converts, Paul reminds them that Abraham had two wives. Then he goes on to tell them that this is an allegory, that these two wives are the two covenants: the old of bondage and slavery, the new of freedom and sonship. The sense that Paul is pointing to here is what some authors call the typological sense. Persons and events of salvation history as it was worked out from the time of Adam until the advent of the Messiah foretell what is to be fulfilled in that messianic age. The theophanies of Moses and Elijah were types of that which the apostles enjoyed on Tabor and which we will all enjoy in the age to come. Jonah's three days in the whale typified Jesus' days in the tomb. Sometimes the type is an anti-type. Eve, mother of all the living, who led us all into sin and death, is an anti-type of Mary, the mother of all who live in Christ, who leads us into holiness and eternal life.

∾   Spiritual Senses   ∾

This divine use of typology—perhaps expanded somewhat by an inspired writer like St. Paul, who tells us that the rock that followed the Chosen People through the desert, supplying them with their needed water, was Christ—opened the way for further development. The Fathers soon enough were speaking of the spiritual senses of Scripture. They saw basically three spiritual senses.

There is what is called the *allegorical* or *mystical sense.* Here the inspired text is open to many deeper meanings, which relate to the ongoing journey of the new chosen people, the Church, and to individuals among them. In this sense we can most readily interpret the stories of the Hebrew Testament, such as the relationship of Cain and Abel or, more happily, that of David and Jonathan. Esther's role in regard to her people tells us some-thing about Mary's role on our behalf. And so on. It is particularly the prophetic and poetic Revelation that is open to rich allegorical interpretation. William of St. Thierry, one of the last of the Fathers, collected whole books of patristic interpretation of the Song of Songs before writing his own *Exposition on the Song of Songs.*

This very humble man tells us in the introduction to his *Exposition* that he will leave the forest of allegory to others and content himself with exposing the *moral sense* of the text. This is considered to be another of the spiritual senses of Scripture, one that tells us what the Text calls us to. It is sometimes called the tropological sense. The exotic descriptions of the relationship between the Bridegroom and the Bride in the Song of Songs not only tell us about the passionate love relationship that God wants to have with us and with his Church, but they also tell us something about how we personally should act in our relationship with God. They certainly invite us to go far beyond the literal do's and don'ts of the commandments. Their challenge is so daring that it could hardly have been expressed in some literal text. It almost has to be expressed in allegory.

Even more so, the ultimate end to which we are called, which eye has not seen, nor ear heard, which has not even entered into the human mind, has to be revealed to us in type and image and allegory. This is the *anagogical or unitive sense* of Scripture: what lies ahead, when in truth all things are ours and we are Christ's and Christ is God's.

By way of a simple example: We read of Jerusalem. Literally, Jerusalem is a city in the Holy Land. Historically, it has played different roles and these might invite different spiritual meanings. Allegorically, Jerusalem can be understood as the Church, which gathers together all the People of God. Morally, this calls us to a certain allegiance to the Church, a certain way of acting as living stones placed upon the foundation of the apostles with Christ as our cornerstone. Anagogically, Jerusalem is that spotless bride descending from the heavens. Each sense opens up many avenues of thought, inviting us to explore more and more deeply the divine plan and the response to which we are called.

As an aid to remembering these different senses, we might relate them to the different steps or stages of lectio and of friendship. Listening to the Sacred Text and getting acquainted with God, we use primarily the literal sense of Scripture. As we carry the Text with us in meditation, we become more friendly with the Lord and the deeper allegorical meanings open out for us. Confident prayer to our Friend is the source and summit of moral response, of a moral life. Finally, as contemplation brings us into union with our Beloved, we begin to understand something of the anagogical or unitive sense.

The Way of Lectio	*The Way of Friendship*	*The Senses of Scripture*
Lectio	Acquaintanceship	Literal
Meditatio	Friendly companionship	Allegorical
Oratio/Prayer	Friendship	Tropological/Moral
Contemplatio	Union	Anagogical/Unitive

I think all of us as we do our lectio tend rather spontaneously to develop the spiritual senses of Scripture. If we have a rather speculative bent of mind, we might tend more toward developing the allegorical or mystical sense. If we are more moralistic in our attitude toward life, we will seek out the moral sense. In order that we do not go astray and draw from the Scriptures misleading or exaggerated "truths," we all need to keep in touch with the literal sense. The spiritual senses can never contradict the literal sense of the text. But it is also good for us to stretch ourselves a bit. If we find that we tend to stay primarily with one sense of Scripture, we would do well to stop and explore what might be the other senses of the Text. It is something like a mother serving up a meal. She will put various kinds of food on the table. Children naturally like one thing more than another. And if they are allowed, they will eat only that particular dish—the meat or the potatoes or the carrots—and ignore the others. Naturally, a mother will insist that the children eat some of each. She does this so that the children will have a balanced diet, but also so that they will grow up enjoying many things, having discovered through their mother's insistence how good they are. Attending to the diverse senses of Scripture can help to keep us in balance with a breadth that embraces the whole Church, a certain depth, a moral fidelity, and a vibrant hope for the future.

This variety will help to keep our lectio really alive and interesting. Actually, I wonder how anyone can ever weary of listening to the Scriptures. They are filled with such a challenging, wondrous, startling, and even scandalous variety: pornographic love songs, shocking stories that outdo any salacious novel, savagery and violence beyond any of today's so-called thrillers, wonders that surpass our fairy tales, embarrassing laws long since outgrown, fantastic (and that is the word) portrayals that make science fiction grow pale, as well as everyday, all-too-familiar stories of life. As Peter of Celles, another writer from that century of the Last of the Fathers, put it: "Our every weariness will be countered by as many varieties of reading as there are moments in our life however long we live."

The Church to some extent gives us sure guidance in interpreting the Scriptures. But as we have seen, even the authoritative teachers of the Church have at times gone astray in their biblical interpretation. Actually there is very little that the Church has taught with infallible authority. That little, of course, is supremely important, such as the teaching as to which are the true books of inspired Scripture. Patristic studies have their place especially here in helping us to enter into the spiritual senses of Scripture in the way that the Spirit has guided the People of God through the centuries. The Fathers share many interpretations with us both in regard to the Church—and Mary who is seen as a type of the

Church—and in regard to ourselves as individual members of Christ the Church.

The Scriptures are love letters from the Lord. It is important that we read between the lines and not miss the communications and intuitions of love. As one of the greatest of the scholastics, Aquinas himself, has said: "Where the mind leaves off, the heart goes beyond."

Chapter Eleven

Lectio in Cyberspace

A few years ago I was asked to bring Centering Prayer to South Africa. I flew the seventeen hours from Hong Kong to New York, and then another seventeen hours to Johannesburg. I was almost immediately taken to one of the black homelands to begin sharing the prayer. Later in the day we toured a school in what had appeared to me to be a fairly primitive place. I was a bit taken aback when we entered the first grade and there were all the little boys and girls, each sitting in front of a very colorful IBM computer! The cybernetic age had reached even this outpost.

We are indeed in a new age. Some compare it with the change that took place with the invention of printing. But in fact that was not as great a transition as that which took place in the middle of the twelfth century. Printing just made more universally available the fruit of that earlier change, when the human family shifted from oral to conceptual communication. Up to the twelfth century, even when readers had a text in front of them, the communication from the inscribed page was not achieved by grasping organized concepts such as words, sentences, and paragraphs. Rather, the letters drawn on the lines were so many phonetic signs that had to be translated into sounds and heard by the ear before they communicated to the human mind. Discovering the alphabet as a technology, even though it had been around for a millennium and more, opened the way to a new kind of communication: the communication of ideas from the words on the page, through the eye, directly to the mind.

Today, as the page is being projected onto a monitor screen, computers can greatly facilitate this kind of communication. We can very legitimately use them for this purpose alone; in fact, many of us older folks will use them largely for this purpose. But if we see this as what the cybernetic age really means, we will be missing the point. As important and as useful as it may be, computers don't simply produce lines of printed text on a screen. Computers also provide a total and increasingly interactive experience.

This is not to deny that computers do present a certain danger to culture and life. They can easily lead one to abandon depth and to become quite shallow, drawing back from the unfathomable depths that Christianity opens out to us, accepting and seeking the illusionary security of lateral connectedness. Actually, for those who do most of their reading from the computer screen, developing lectio on the computer can invite a new dimension of depth to enter into this constantly increasing lateral expansion. We want to approach the new technology with open eyes and hearts. All things are ours, and we are Christ's.

Those of us who love books and find something good and reassuring about having a book in our hands do not need to fear that the book is coming to the end of its two-millennium history. Mega-bookstores proclaim the opposite. But we cannot ignore the fact that within the walls of these mammoth buildings, along with a million books, there are not just comfortable chairs, quiet corners, and cups of fragrant coffee, but also thousands of compact disks and tapes, software of all sorts, TV screens, and computers. Many of our precious books are laid out in a way that more resembles the computer screen than the printed page of yore. And for every mega-bookstore there is probably more than one cyber café.

It certainly would be foolish of us, especially in the name of authentic lectio, to close ourselves to or to reject the abundance of products pouring out of the cornucopia of cybernetics. For ourselves, we can begin to use its products to our own advantage. For the future, we need to face the challenge it offers for the sake of our commitment to Christ and his will to bring the Good News effectively to today's children.

It is widely known that many complete versions of the Bible are available on the Web. (Try http://www.csbsju.edu/osb/gen/topics/lectio for a start. This site also offers a rich selection of patristic texts.) There is no reason why we, as well as our youngsters, cannot sit in front of the computer screen to do our lectio, if we are comfortable with that. Whole Bibles are available, as well as liturgical lectionaries and daily selections. We can call up several translations of the Bible and have them on parallel screens so that we can easily see several translations at the same time. With the click of the mouse, cross-references can be invited in to enrich our reading. We can turn to the Greek or Hebrew texts and with the help of the dictionaries and commentaries available come into more immediate contact with the original text. Encyclopedias are available to help us get the wider historical context of any text.

If we want to enrich our hearing with associated texts, there are concordances and search engines to find all such texts. For example, when I hear Jesus say, "the Blood of the new covenant," I can search into the many texts in the Hebrew Bible that speak of the covenant and of blood and get more of a sense as to what Jesus, who was thoroughly familiar with those texts and who was speaking out of that context, is saying to us. Another click of the mouse can bring up a commentary on any text I have highlighted.

With all of this, of course, we have to be careful that our lectio does not turn into study. Or that we don't end up just satisfying our curiosity. It is important that we do keep clear just what lectio is: a meeting with the Lord in and through his Word. But the literal sense with its historical meaning is the basis for such a meeting, even as it invites us into a rich allegorical interaction.

The World Wide Web also opens up to us the possibility of a far richer Bible sharing. Our group now can meet without our ever stirring from our homes. It can easily include the handicapped and others who cannot leave their homes. And it can reach out and include participants from other parts of the world and other cultures. This can add a tremendous richness to the sharing. We might be fortunate enough to bring into our group a person who lives in the Holy Land, a person who lives a traditional Jewish life, a person who knows the biblical languages and/or the history of the times, or one who has studied the archeological finds or the Dead Sea Scrolls. It is amazing whom we can meet on the Internet. Young people around the world are eager to communicate and will enter into conversation on almost anything.

It is a sad reality that it is the pornographic industry that has gotten the largest bite of the Web so far. But it does not have to remain that way. Each and every one of us can make our own contribution to filling the Web with the Good News. I have an

Orthodox friend who has put a computer in his prayer room at home (actually a corner of his basement). Each night, after his family retires, he goes there, prays for a time, and then goes on the Web and enters into conversation wherever he finds an opening. Not just on the Orthodox bulletin boards, though he could spend his full time there. For him, it means giving up some sleep. But he has brought the Good News to many. And he has found the truth of the old adage: the best way to learn is to teach. As he has shared with others, Holy Spirit has tremendously enriched his own understanding and love for his faith.

Computer lectio can be a special blessing for the sight impaired. With just a click of the mouse we can elevate the text from

ten point

to

twenty

or

forty

or more! Thus any text that can be found on the computer can be read easily.

It doesn't have to stop there. Optelec[1] and other companies have produced fairly simple machines that will read any book into our computer. There are

also machines that operate independent of computers. So, as long as we can see, we can go right on
doing lectio by reading.

And even if, God forbid, our sight goes altogether,
in this technological age we can still listen to the
Word of God and any other helpful book we want.
Although nothing can surpass the warmth and
intimacy of a human reader, a machine we can
independently operate does give us a freedom that
we would not otherwise have. The Xavier Society for
the Blind and other groups provide an abundance of
good books and magazines on tapes. Xerox has
developed "The Reading Edge."[2] There is an easy-
to-use help system that speaks all instruction aloud.
It reads from 40 to 550 words a minute, has nine
different voices, reads italics and bold different ways,
repeats words and sentences at the push of a button,
and so on. It is a lightweight machine that fits into a
briefcase. All in all, it is an invitation to return to that
earlier time when lectio was, even for the reader, a
question of *hearing* the Word of God.

I think a parish community should be sure that
any of its members who need this kind of technological help to be able to do their lectio should be
provided with it. This assistance could also include
the possibility of computer communication for those
who are not able to move beyond their homes to
take part in parish life. Gifts along this line would be
another way in which more affluent communities
could help others less fortunate.

Besides text, though, I think we can be helped
with the richness of graphics that are readily available on computers—far more than any home library
could ever hope to contain in a private library. We
can be taken for tours by outstanding scholars and
hear as well as see the biblical environment. Jesus
extensively used the images of his environment:
farmers, vines, fig tree, mustard seed, shepherds and
sheep. Think of what a blessing these graphics
might be for, say, an Eskimo who has never seen a
field sown or sheep on the hillside, or for a lad from
the plains who has never seen the angry sea or
fishermen pulling in nets. These lasting impressions
can enrich all our future lectio.

Dramatic presentations also have their value.
Parents should take care that even while their little
ones see *The Lion King* twenty-two times, presentations of the stories of Jesus and the story of Jesus,
as well as the wonderful stories from the Hebrew
Bible, are also on the menu. While the children are
very young, the colorful cartoon-type of presentation
might be best. Later, more serious dramatic presentation is needed. Hollywood has made some contri-
butions here. But much more needs to be done. I
think we who have heard our Lord's command to
"go forth and teach all" have a real obligation here.
If our young people are going to hear the Good
News effectively, they are going to have to get it
through the CD-ROM, videocassette, and other up-
to-date means of communication. A whole new

generation of translators is going to have to be cultivated and supported—men and women who have benefited from the best of biblical studies and are themselves products of the cybernetic age. They will know how to communicate in the media of this rapidly evolving age. All this work can't be accomplished in any one year, but it does need to be begun and pursued as quickly as possible. From everywhere I hear the lament that we are losing the young people. We are! And if we don't get to work and get out on the cutting edge of communication, the Good News will never be heard by those who are to lead this world tomorrow.

We should not be prudish in our biblical presentations. There is an immense amount of sex in the Bible, sex of all kinds. We could, at best and with immense effort, shield our young people only for a relatively short time from knowledge of the diverse and perverse sexual activity that is prevalent in our modern world. Best it be presented to them straightforwardly in the biblical context in which God has had his inspired writers speak about it. Father Andrew Greeley has been highly criticized by many for his novels. I have not seen most of them, but I was struck by his attempt in *The Love Story* to place his story into a biblical context, a contemporary paraphrase of Solomon's Song of Songs. It's an attempt to put some of today's reality with all its dilemmas into the context of some of the values and principles that have helped human beings through the centuries to work through such universal struggles. I do not know how well Father Greeley succeeds in what he is trying to do, but I think there is some validity to his approach. The abstract enunciation of principles, no matter how many biblical quotations we might be able to bring forth to "prove" them, is not going to go very far with most of us today. There is something richly human in the way the Fathers generally presented the values and principles of Judeo-Christian life, and that compassionate reality is called for today. I don't think it has to be humanistic to the degree that it loses its theistic centering. The more integral communication potential of today's media and of the media that is rapidly evolving offers us an opportunity to bring the Good News in a much more powerful way than the printed page and the scholastic outlook has afforded us. But it is time and past time for those whose lives are about evangelization to seize the initiative.

All of us who are alive today are part of the cybernetic age. Unless we are shielding ourselves with an extremely rigid listening, the age is penetrating our listening and enlarging it in its own ways. It is important for us to acknowledge this and to harness these new potentialities in our life in order to move more powerfully and effectively toward the goals we have set for ourselves and for which we are made by God, and in which lie our true happiness. This potential needs to be integrated into our lectio listening or our listening for God, and the message of God, will gradually be squeezed as we hear more and more that which is being beamed at us by the world in ways that are more compatible with our evolving cybernetic listening. If we harness and foster this new potential in the listening that we are for hearing the Word, there is every promise that as grace works with nature, our lectio will become more and more effective in bringing about the transformation of consciousness that we so want as we seek the mind and heart of Christ. And we will grow in our ability to contribute to bringing the Good News effectively to the next generation.

N.B. Although names, addresses, and phone numbers may have changed since publication, you might try to find further information by starting here:

[1]Optelec
 6 Lyberty Way
 Westford, MA 01886
 800-828-1056

[2]The Reading Edge
 Telesensory OCR Products Division
 520 Almanor Avenue
 Sunnyvale, CA 94086-3533
 800-804-8004

Chapter Twelve

Listening Together

In an earlier chapter I spoke of an occasion when I brought into our community meeting a book that I had covered partly in red and partly in green. When I asked the brethren what color it was, one of the wiser brethren responded: *"As far as I can see,* it is green." It is very important for us to realize that each of us has only a limited, a very limited, listening. We perceive only a part of the reality that is presented to us—a very small part, infinitesimally small, when the reality is the Reality.

This is certainly one reason for wanting to enter into shared lectio. Each participant in a shared lectio has his or her perception. Small though our respective perceptions may be, they certainly augment the

total perception of each when they are added together. My perception of the green side of the cover
is filled out by my brother's perception of the red
side. Other reports will tell us that the spine of the
cover is white. And because each one of us gathered
together to listen to the Word brings to the experience our own unique listening, we each have something unique to share with the others.

My experience is that people really enjoy sharing
lectio. They enjoy being able to make their own
unique contribution. At the same time, they enjoy
seeing their perception enlarged and enriched,
complemented in many ways as different individuals
in the group add their perceptions.

This enrichment in itself would be enough to make
us really want to be part of a lectio sharing group. But
there are other advantages that can motivate us. If I
have a commitment to meet each day with another to
share lectio, it is much more likely that I will indeed be
faithful to the daily practice of lectio. Even if I belong
to a group that meets only weekly, my faithfulness will
be supported. There will be a certain sense of accountability to the group. I will be letting them down
as well as letting myself down and failing my Lord if I
am not faithful to my daily meeting with him.

And then there is the wonderful bonding that takes
place—something like what happened for the Twelve
our Lord gathered around himself. As we meet
regularly and share more and more openly what
touches the deepest part of our life—our relationship

with our God—our sense of oneness and of being in this together will necessarily grow. Care, love, concern, compassion: we will be there for each other. We will know support, understanding, friendship.

I really wonder if there is anything that can contribute more to a happy and fulfilled marriage and family life than daily shared lectio. How good it would be if this were to be a regular part of pre-marriage counseling or marriage preparation: that the couple would be introduced to shared lectio. At the wedding itself the pastor could present the newlyweds with their family Bible. And soon after, as they set up house, he could come and enthrone that Bible in their home.

So many parents today lament that their children have drifted away from the faith. Perhaps these young men and women have never had a real faith experience, have not experienced the faith as something vitally alive and meaningful in their family life. If, from earliest memories, they could recall their parents sitting down together as disciples of Jesus, listening to what he had to say to them for that day, receiving a word of life—if they were drawn into this sharing from an early age—would not the story be quite different? This daily sharing does not have to be a very demanding event. I have spoken before of my aunt and uncle, who open breakfast each day with a word from the Gospel. A family that has to get off to work and get children out to school might not find breakfast a good time, though one would hope that some time is given to morning prayer,

consecrating the day to the Lord. At the beginning
or end of the evening meal might be a good time. If
a family does not regularly sit down and do something together, there is little hope that that family will
continue to be in any way a meaningful family once
the children break away. Parents who do not nurture
family as the children grow up can expect an
uncared-for and lonely old age. But a family that is
together regularly in the experience of Jesus' love
for them, and family members who share openly
among themselves their joys and sorrows in living
the Christ-life, will experience a bond of love growing that will last into eternal life.

The family is and will always remain the basic,
God-constituted unit of a healthy society. Sad to say,
though, a happy, loving, well-bonded family, centered on the Lord and in his love, is becoming more
and more rare. And the tragic results in our cities
and in our world are only too painfully evident. A
powerful and effective effort to remedy this human
tragedy being undertaken in varying degrees in
different parts of the Christian world today is the
base community. It is within these communities that
the power of shared lectio most effectively shines
forth in our times. These groups have turned to
Jesus present in his Word as the vitalizing core and
center of their community. Their ever-deeper bonding as community grows out of their shared lectio,
and it is the source and guide of their community
action as well. Daily they gather to listen, to share,

and to discern. They carry this practice home into
their individual families. Christ in his Word is everywhere present in their lives, a Real Presence that
strengthens, supports, and gives meaning to lives
that oftentimes would otherwise be unbearable. Base
communities may be primarily flourishing among the
very poor and disenfranchised, where the wounds of
society lay more exposed. But the need is as great in
suburbia, where alcoholism, drugs, marital infidelity,
divorce, and suicide betray the mask of respectability. There is little hope for our society at any level if
there is no heart at the center of it. And that heart
has to be the all-loving heart of a God who can
heal and make whole and give infinite meaning to
lives that cry from their very being for such mean-
ingfulness.

Sharing lectio can be done very simply indeed.
Two or more sit down together and open the Bible.
The steps of the method of lectio described earlier
are followed: They take a moment to be aware of
God's presence in his Word. They ask Holy Spirit to
help them hear. They listen to the Word and respond in their hearts. They might decide then to
share what they are hearing, or they might want first
to choose the word they are going to carry with
them and to thank the Lord for it before they begin
to share with each other. Either way is fine. They
may read from the one Bible, or they may each have
a Bible. One may read aloud, and the others listen.
All may read the same passage, or each may choose

her or his own. There are many possibilities, and each family, each group, can decide for itself.

When I am conducting Centering Prayer Prayer-shops, I usually invite each person to take up his or her own Bible. After coming into Presence and calling upon the Spirit, each chooses a passage to listen to. After five minutes I invite them to choose a word to take from the experience and then thank the Lord. After another minute or so I invite them to share their experience of God in the lectio with the person sitting next to them. This way, no matter what size the group is, the sharing can be done with the least amount of commotion. I usually give them about four minutes for the sharing, though it is often difficult to get them to stop. People do enjoy sharing! Then, before I allow them to ask me any questions about lectio, *I* ask *them* a question: "Did you share with your partner some of the thoughts, ideas, and insights you got while listening to the Lord, or did you—as I asked you—share with your partner your experience of God during the lectio?" At his point I usually get a bit of stunned silence and then a big "Ohhh!" They get the point. Lectio is primarily being with the Lord, experiencing his presence. He may or may not give us some real insight during any particular period of lectio. It certainly is a gift if he does. But the important thing is being with him. We have to be careful, especially when there is going to be a shar-ing, not to turn lectio into an intellectual exercise, a quest for bright ideas. It is letting a Friend be with us, communicating with us through his Word, whether or not what he does communicate adds up to anything more than loving chatter.

For most shared lectio, whether in a family or in a group—whether a lectio- or Bible-sharing group, a Centering Prayer group or any other kind of group that wants its being together to be enriched by this significant presence of the Lord—I think the simpler the structure, the better. However, some more elaborate approaches to group lectio have been developed. This is especially true among base communities where the group depends on shared lectio not only for its cohesion as a group but also for discerning its course of action. I will share one such approach here, not so much as an endorsement of this particular approach but as an example which can open up ideas for a group that would like to experiment with a richer structure.

This particular method is largely that of Doug and Norvene Vest, Oblates of Saint Andrew's Abbey, Valyermo. It has been presented at the Benedictine Spirituality for Laity Workshop conducted at the abbey each summer. I take responsibility for the way it is presented here, not pretending to faithfully present the Vests' ideas in every detail. Indeed, I bring something of my own approach to it.

This particular method works best with groups of four to eight. Much larger groups would need to be divided. Each group would then choose a leader, who would with the group select the Scripture passage to be used, nominate the readers, watch the time, and lead the prayer.

The group gathers around the enthroned Text and spends a bit of time in quieting adoration, disposing themselves to hear the Lord. The leader calls upon Holy Spirit to help them in this hearing, expanding their listening and making their listening more supple.

This particular method actually calls for the same passage to be read aloud four times by three different readers, the first reader reading the passage twice. Reading always involves an interpretation, so the readers do contribute significantly to the group's experience of the Word. In a mixed group it would be good to alternate the readers between the sexes.

The first double reading has as its purpose the real hearing of the passage and receiving from it a "word" (in the classical sense, a word, phrase, or short sentence) that touches the heart. Once the word is received or chosen, we each gently repeat our word, allowing its message to unfold within. After the second reading the group abides in silence for a couple of minutes, each nurturing the word we have received. Then, beginning with the leader and moving around the circle, we each share the word we have been pondering—and nothing more for the moment.

The text is now read again by another person. This time we are each listening to the Lord speaking directly to us. Where does this word touch our lives today? What is the Lord saying to us now through this word? After a couple of minutes of silence

during which we each ponder this question, we have
the opportunity to share briefly with the group what
we are hearing from the Lord, what insight he is
giving us now.

There is then a final reading, the same passage by
yet another member of our group. This time we are
seeking to experience what the Lord is calling us
forth to do or to be through this word he has spoken
to us—and to do now, this day or this week. In this
meeting with the Lord he calls us in some way to
make him more present in our world, to bring him in
some way to our world for its healing. Again, after a
bit of quiet reflection, we each have the opportunity
to share what we sense ourselves called to. However,
here, as before, we can abide in silence if we do not
feel ready to share.

It is now time for prayer. The challenges may be
great. The leader may invite each of us to pray in a
special way for the person to our right and to continue to hold that person in special prayer as he or
she seeks to live out what the Lord has called forth.

It is possible to relate these three stages in this
lectio experience with three of the senses of Scripture we have seen above. The first would be listening
for the literal sense. The second would be seeking to
personalize the Word by a listening for the allegorical
sense. And finally, the call to action would be a
moral sense. We could, of course, add a fourth stage
that would look to what this is going to lead to. This
would be a source of hope and consolation.

Let me now try to present this approach in a more concise form:

∿ *Shared Lectio* ∿

The group gathers around the enthroned Text in quieting adoration and calls upon Holy Spirit for help.

1. *Reading:* One person reads aloud a chosen passage from the Scriptures and after a pause reads it a second time. All listen, attentive to the Lord now speaking to them.
   Silence: Each allows a chosen word or phrase from the reading quietly to repeat itself within.
   Sharing: Each one shares the word or phrase, without any elaboration.

2. *Reading:* Another member of the group now reads the same passage.
   Silence: Each one now reflects for a couple of minutes, asking, "What has the Lord said to me in this reading with regard to my life today?"
   Sharing: Each may share briefly: "I hear the Lord saying to me . . . "

3. *Reading:* Another member of the group reads the passage again.
   Silence: Now each reflects for a couple of minutes on "I believe the Lord wants me to . . . today/this week."

Sharing: Each may share what came forth in the course of his or her reflection.

At the end of the sharing there is a time of silent prayer. Each may pray in a special way for the person to his or her right. The leader then invites all to rise and pray together the Lord's Prayer.

Please remember that this somewhat complicated method is offered only to open up possibilities and to invite each group to use its freedom. We can explore what actually helps us as a group to encounter the Lord and to share that encounter among ourselves and bring it back into our lives. The basic values of an enriched hearing, support in fidelity to practice, and a deepening bonding in the love of Christ are what is important in shared lectio. The method or approach, whatever it may be, is totally in the service of these values. Where the Spirit is, there is freedom. Indeed, a regular practice of lectio will usually lead us to a great freedom in sharing with others what we are receiving from the Lord, whether it is in a structured setting or just spontaneously through the day. The Word will become more and more our word, readily on our lips, expressing in one way or another the growing love we have for each of our sisters and brothers, a participation in Christ's great love for each one.

Epilogue

Mary: The Reader
and the Book

Those devoted to the holy virgin Mary often lament that there is so little about her in the Bible. And they are right in a sense, though she is to be found from one end of the Sacred Text to the other. She is the Woman promised by God in Genesis and crowned by him in Revelation. She is found in type and anti-type in the Hebrew Bible. Her words and appear-ances in the Gospels add up to a complete modeling of Christian discipleship. We can all join with her cousin Elizabeth in declaring: "Blessed is she who believed. . . . "

Mary certainly heard the Word and had an amaz-ing listening for it. Let us just for a moment be with one of her experiences insofar as we can. Here is this young woman—we would think of her as not much more than a girl—who has lived all her life in an end-of-the-road mountain village. (Can anything good come out of Nazareth?) Everything in town centered on the synagogue, where they heard the Word of God, chanted it, filled their minds and hearts with it. If one were fortunate enough to learn to read and write, it was from the Bible. The glory of these Jewish people was that they were the Chosen People, that there was but one God, and he was their God, Yahweh, a name too sacred to be pronounced.

Then one day—we don't know what Mary was doing at the moment—an angel walked into her life. Perhaps this was not as startling an experience for her as it might have been for us, for all her life she had heard of angels coming to her Father Abraham and others of her people. The angel's salutation did disturb her, for she was a humble maid, not used to extravagant praise. But then the angel went on to tell her that Yahweh has a Son. There was absolutely nothing in her listening that could have prepared her for such a revelation. And the angel went further: Yahweh wants you to be the mother of that Son.

We don't know how much Mary understood of what was being revealed to her. In essence she heard for the first time the two fundamental truths of the Christian faith: the Trinity and the Incarnation. We do know she understood sufficiently to give an informed consent to what God was asking of her. In fact, she made sure she had sufficient understanding of what she was being asked before she gave her consent. She did not hesitate to question the divine messenger. Though the words might have been similar, the spirit of her questioning was very different from that of her cousin's husband, Zachary. Hers was already filled with faith. She sought to know more only in order to be able to respond fully to the divine will.

With a supple listening that was able under the influence of the overshadowing Spirit to expand incredibly, Mary heard the Word and received the Word, even physically, into her being. She allowed the Word to be so present in her that her mere presence, her word of greeting, brought sanctification and prophetic joy.

Luke tells us that Mary "pondered" all these things in her heart. That is a pregnant word: *ponder.* (One of the newer translations came up with, "Mary thought all these things over." I almost threw the Sacred Text out the window—Lord, forgive me!) The word "ponder" has the sense about it of allowing the Word to rest within and of its own gravity to form and shape and expand the knowledge of the heart. It is like a seal placed on soft wax. Resting there gently, it of its own weight conforms the wax to its image and likeness.

Mary's whole life had been and continued to be a reading of the Word, in an ever-more-intimate and incarnate sense. It had its dark moments. There were days of searching Jerusalem, only to hear, "Did you not know I must be about my Father's business?" The Lord is always present to us. But if he does leave us at times with a sense of loss, it is only because he is about his Father's business of forming us into perfect lovers.

Mary did not hesitate to speak up, when there was need: "They have no wine."

Soon after this her Son would say to the crowd: "Don't be like the pagans who think that they will be heard because of their many words. Your Father knows what you need before you ask him."

"Pray thus: 'Father, . . . thy will be done.'"

And Mary told the servants: "Do whatever he tells you."

One day Mary with a number of the Lord's brethren approached the place where he was teaching. As was usual in those days of his ministry, he was mobbed. Word was passed in through the mob: "Your mother is outside."

"And who is my mother?" asked Jesus. "The one who does the will of my Father in heaven."

"Yes," said Mary, "do whatever he tells you."

A woman from the crowd shouted out, as only a woman could have: "Blessed is the womb that bore you and the breasts that nursed you."

"Yea," said the Lord, "rather blessed is the one who has heard the Word of the God and keeps it."

It was not always easy, but Mary entered more and more deeply into the mystery of the Incarnation. The pondering of years, as she saw a seemingly

quite ordinary child grow under her maternal care,
was challenged by the wonder of her boy working
miracles and being acclaimed by mobs. Yet at that
last moment he was a caring and dutiful son. Even
as the skies darkened and tombs opened and the veil
of the Temple was torn asunder and a Gentile
proclaimed him the Son of God, he concerned
himself about her care and her need to love: "Son,
behold your mother. Mother, behold your Son."

God liked to draw wonderful word pictures for us
in his inspired writings. Indeed, the whole of creation is a wonderful picture drawn by God to tell us
of his love and care for us. The early Christian
community was not slow in extracting these pictures
and tracing them on the walls of their catacombs.
Soon enough they were being reproduced on pieces
of carefully prepared wood. There was a great
controversy over these icons, as they were called,
but the wisdom and grace of the Incarnation pre-
vailed and icons became a hallowed part of the
Christian tradition. Within this tradition of the icon
there is a collection of sixteen festal icons depicting
key events in the lives of Jesus and Mary. While
leaving scope for the talent of the individual artist,
each of the sixteen has its own set pattern.

The icon of the Annunciation always shows Mary
reading the Scriptures. It was precisely her lifelong
searching of the Scriptures that prepared her to
receive the new revelation the angel came to bring

her. In the icon of the Annunciation the angel himself bears a scroll. As he proclaims the Good News to Mary, she seems to continue her reading. It is as if all he had to say to her she was already finding in the Sacred Text. Indeed, the angel appeals to what Mary has been reading about David and his Son.

Mary had learned to read at her mother's knee from the Sacred Texts. In time, she too would teach her Son at her knee to read from them. Jesus is primarily the Book, but he too was a reader, as was so evident on the path to Emmaus and so many other times in his discourse and prayer. Mary is the reader preeminent, reading the Book of the Scriptures and the Book that is her Son. She, in turn, becomes a book for us, where we can learn how to read her Son, who became most readable for us through Mary at the Incarnation. We in our turn must become a book—after we have been prepared like parchment for the inscription of the Word—so that Jesus can be written in us. We are to be books in which all who meet us can read Jesus and his love, which is God. For God is love.

Mary saw what she read in the prophecies fulfilled in her own life. It was a source of joy and consolation and at the same time a source of mounting dread. This young woman did conceive and bear a Son who is called Emmanuel, God with us. A star did rise out of Bethlehem. After the horror of exile, God did call his Son out of Egypt back to the peace of Nazareth. But the Songs of the Suffering Servant

were a dirge in her heart, orchestrated by the prophetic words of old Simeon.

The Presentation at the Temple is another icon in
the series. As disciples of Jesus, we too see fulfilled
in our lives what has been foretold by Simeon and
Jesus and his disciples. And while this fulfillment is a
source of immense joy and hope, there is the dread,
for we must take up our daily cross and, like the
grain of wheat, fall to the ground and die.

Mary's wonderful hymn, which we call the
Magnificat, is an ample witness to her reading of the
Scriptures, to her pondering upon them and coming
to a fuller understanding of them through her own
experience. She sets forth a biblical wisdom that her
Son's people yet struggle to understand, the Good
News of liberation:

> He has put down the mighty from their
> thrones
> and has exalted the humble.
> He has filled the hungry with good things
> and sent the rich away empty.

Mary's growth in understanding was a gradual
process. At the Annunciation she questioned. She
did not understand the full import of what her Son
said to her in his doings and words when he first
exercised his manhood at the age of twelve. At times
she did not understand, but she always kept the faith
and acted in faith. Her faith-filled journey across the
hills to her cousin Elizabeth was rewarded with

reassuring prophecy. Holy Spirit had overshadowed her and remained with her, enlightening her understanding. At Cana she approached her Son with a certain sureness and unwavering faith: "Do whatever he tells you."

Mary is indeed a model for us: accepting in faith, searching and questioning in faith, pondering, acting in obedience, willing to wait in silence, always depending on Holy Spirit. Mary is the reader par excellence. And in the book that she is, we can best learn how to read and do our own lectio.

Mary was a hearer of the Word. Nowhere has the Word that was most fully expressed in Jesus Christ been so fully and faithfully received than in the person and life of the holy Virgin. She kept it and pondered it in her heart. Her whole being was a most attentive listening, a wide open, completely supple listening, until she was able to be fully in union with her Son on Calvary's hill, to enter into the silence of a new holy Sabbath, and to remain forever in the midst of the Church at prayer.

Not much of what Mary said has been recorded for us to read, but what has been given us is enough to fully guide the life of a disciple of Christ. As is always the case, she spoke more by who she is and what she did.

> *And he that is mighty has done great*
> *things for her.*
> *And holy is his name.*

APPENDICES

Appendix One

Enthroning the Sacred Scriptures in the Home

In many churches today the Sacred Scriptures are enthroned in a place of honor, open and readily available to any who would approach to receive a "word." In the Abbey church at Spencer, Massachusetts (and I am sure in many other places), two lamps are always burning: one before the tabernacle proclaiming the Real Presence in the Eucharist, the other over the Bible in the middle of the community proclaiming the Real Presence of the Lord in his Word. This is fully in accord with the renewal called forth by Holy Spirit through the Second Vatican Council. In the *Decree on Divine Revelation* the Council Fathers clearly spoke of the similarity of these sacraments of the Real Presence:

> The Church has always venerated the divine
> Scriptures just as it venerates the Body of the
> Lord, since from the table of both the Word of

God and the Body of Christ it unceasingly
receives and offers to the faithful the Bread of
Life. . . . In the sacred Books, the Father who
is in heaven meets his children with great love
and speaks with them.

It follows naturally that the Scriptures, when
reverenced in the home, are a constant reminder of
God's Presence and blessing. A formal "enthronement" of the family Bible is a wonderful way to
begin this custom in your own home. It is good if the
pastor of the local parish can lead this rite, but he
may delegate another, perhaps the head of the
household. The enthroning of the Bible may take
place at the same time as the blessing of the home.

At an appropriate time family and friends gather.
After a suitable welcome is given to all, the
presider begins.

Presider: Peace be to this house and all who dwell
herein.

The presider may then sprinkle the house with
holy water or proceed with the blessing of the
house, if this is also to be done at the same time.
   Then all gather at the place where the Sacred
Scriptures are to be enthroned. For this occasion
the chosen place should be suitably adorned with
flowers and candles, if possible. The Bible to be

enthroned is placed on a table before the place of enthronement. Most properly it is the family Bible, but it might be a Bible presented to the family by the parish on this occasion.

The presider then speaks to those gathered in the following or similar words:

Presider: This is a very special moment for this house and for all who dwell here, for at this moment the Lord is coming into your midst to be present with you in a special way. God is always with us, living in our hearts and abiding among us when we are together in his love. But God dwells in a very special way in his Word. He comes in his Word to speak to us, to tells us of his love and care, to give us sure guidance for our journey towards our heavenly home, our true and lasting home. Let us welcome the Lord now, listen to him, speak to him, and receive his blessing.

At this time the group may sing a welcoming hymn such as "We Gather Together," "Come, Holy Ghost," or "Kum Ba Yah." At the end of the hymn the presider blesses the Bible, if it has not yet been blessed.

Presider: Lord, we humbly ask you to bless this book made sacred by the presence of

your holy and life-giving Word. May it be
for us a sacrament, proclaiming that you
abide in our midst, ever ready to speak to
us words of life, of hope, and of love.
May we always hold this book in reverence and benefit constantly by its presence with us. We ask this, Lord, through
Jesus Christ, our Savior and Teacher.

All: Amen.

Presider: Let us be seated now and listen to what
the Lord has to say to us.

*Each member of the family will now read the
passage that he or she has selected for the occasion. At the end of each reading, pause briefly for
reflection. After the last reading, pause for a
longer period. Then the presider invites those
present to share what they have heard.*

Presider: What have you heard the Lord saying to
us today?

*Allow a reasonable amount of time for different
participants to share what they heard as they
listened to the Word being read. Then the presider
leads the group in prayer.*

Presider: Let us now make known our concerns.
[Pause.] First of all, let us thank the Lord
for coming into our midst and speaking
to us today.

All: We thank you, O Lord.

Presider: Let us pray that the Lord will always be welcome in this home and be a real Presence in the lives of all who dwell here.

All: We pray to the Lord.

Presider: Let us pray that all who enter this house as guests will be welcomed by the family and blessed by this Presence in their midst.

All: We pray to the Lord.

Presider: Let us pray that each one of us may be renewed in our faith in the Real Presence of the Lord in his Word and be faithful disciples regularly listening to the Lord in his Word.

All: We pray to the Lord.

Presider: Let us pray that the Church might become an ever more effective minister of the Word, bringing the Good News to all.

All: We pray to the Lord.

Presider: Let us pray that the Word may spread rapidly across the earth bringing peace and hope to all.

All: We pray to the Lord.

Presider: Let us pray that all those who have gone from us may by this holy Word be lead into the joys of their eternal home.

All: We pray to the Lord.

Presider: And for what else shall we pray?

At this point each participant is welcome to put forth any prayers he or she would like the group to join in offering.

Presider:	Let us pray for all the sick, the lonely, the old, for those in prison camps, the deportees and exiles, for those suffering right now from deadly hunger and from war, for those suffering from AIDS and those caring for them, for the dying and the souls in purgatory, for the whole human family.
All:	We pray to the Lord.
Presider:	Lord of love and mercy, we ask you to hear our prayers. Grant all that you know is good for us. Above all, fill us with your Holy Spirit. We ask this through Christ, our Lord.
All:	Amen.
Presider:	And may almighty God bless us, Creator, Savior, and Spirit.
All:	Amen.

The rite may conclude with a suitable hymn, such as "Holy God, We Praise Thy Name" or "Hail, Holy Queen." Then all are invited to partake in appropriate refreshments.

Let us now be attentive to the word of God —

The Method of Lectio

Keeping the Sacred Scriptures enthroned in our home in a place of honor as a Real Presence of the Word in our midst, we benefit by the daily practice of lectio.

1. Take the Sacred Text with reverence and call upon Holy Spirit.

2. For ten minutes (or longer, if you are so drawn), listen to the Lord speaking to you through the Text and respond to him.

3. At the end of the time, choose a word or phrase (perhaps one will have been "given" to you) to take with you, and thank the Lord for being with you and speaking to you.

More briefly, we might put it this way:

- Come into the Presence and call upon Holy Spirit.
- Listen (read or hear) a portion of Scripture for ten minutes.
- Thank the Lord and take a "Word."

APPENDIX THREE

Centering Prayer

Sit relaxed and quiet.

1. Be in faith and love to God who dwells in the center of your being.
2. Take up a love word and let it be gently present, supporting your being to God in faith-filled love.
3. Whenever you become aware of anything, simply and gently return to the Lord with the use of your prayer word.

After twenty minutes let the Our Father (or some other prayer) pray itself.

More briefly, we might put it this way:

- Be with God within.
- Use a word to stay.
- Use the word to return.

The living tradition within which Centering Prayer can be found provides several different ways to practice it, each with its own approach to the riches of grace awaiting the pray-er. One other way of describing the process that is familiar to most practitioners of Centering Prayer is this four-step procedure:

1. Choose a sacred word as the symbol of your intention to consent to God's presence and action within.

2. Sitting comfortably and with eyes closed, settle briefly, and silently introduce the sacred word as the symbol of your consent to God's presence and action within us.

3. When you become aware of anything, return ever-so-gently to God, using the sacred word.

4. At the end of the prayer period, remain in silence with eyes closed for a couple of minutes.

Lectio Vere Divina

Note: These "words of life" were sent to all the monks and nuns of the Cistercian Order of the Strict Observance (Trappists) by their Father General, Father Bernardo Olivera, o.c.s.o. They bring out, with a challenging wisdom that invites one to go deeper and deeper, the many aspects of lectio. May they invite the readers of this volume to bring what they have read to an ever-deeper and more enriching understanding.

I want to spare you the fatigue and annoyance of a long and wide-ranging document. For this reason I have written what follows in the form of brief maxims or *sententiae*. I trust that this will prove more profitable and, perhaps, more pedagogical.

I follow in this the examples of the ancient spiritual writers. Many of them were accustomed to draft their works in sentence-form, each conveying a central theme. The sentence is a brief and succinct saying offering advice and a rule for living, or shows forth doctrine, morals, and good sense, and, in the best examples, wisdom. But for the sentence to convey wisdom it is necessary that he who writes and they who read feel and savor the taste of what they do and live.

∾ *Prelude* ∾

1. The Spirit inspired the Scriptures; therefore, she is present and speaks through them. If she breathes in, she also breathes out.

2. The Scriptures breathe life by the inspiration of the Spirit; that is why they are the breath of the Christian.

3. All of this living book converges on Christ. The Divine Scriptures are one book only: Christ. He is the concise, living, and efficacious Word.

4. All Scripture points to the mystery of Christ: prefigured in the Hebrew Bible and present in the New Testament, interiorized by each Christian and consummated in glory.

5. Because God is infinite, his Word is also infinite: Scripture enshrines infinite mysteries; its meaning is unfathomable.

6. The literal meaning of the text is always the point of departure; the letter reveals the deeds and presents the persons; history is the foundation.

7. The Spirit takes us beyond the letter; our theological life opens the doors of meaning to us:

- Allegorical, building faith through the discovery of Christ and his Church.

- Tropological, teaching us to act in the truth of love.

- Anagogical, showing us and drawing us towards that for which we yearn.

8. The Gospel is the mouth of Christ, ever ready to offer to us the kiss of eternity.

9. The Gospel is the body and blood of Christ, to pray and live is to eat and drink it.

10. The Gospel is the power of God because it shows us the way and gives us the strength to follow it.

11. Herein is found true life, and my spirit neither has nor desires anything but the prayerful reading of these mysteries!

12. The Church is the only sounding-board of the Word of God. Because it is the body of Christ, it is also the Word. Scripture gives us life in the Spirit when received in the ambitus of tradition and the magisterium.

13. Our *Lectio Divina* should prolong the profound meaning of the Word beyond the Liturgy in order to prepare us for a more fruitful celebration of the same.

14. Christians understand the profound meaning of the Word only when living in communion and concord with their brothers and sisters.

15. Our lives should create a biblical climate allowing each and all to be protagonists in the dialogue of salvation.

16. The *humus* of humility is the good soil in which the Word produces abundant fruit.

17. We receive only when we are recollected; only in silence is heard the beating of the heart of God.

18. We speak to God when we pray with love; we hear God when we read his Word with faith.

19. When we are "nailed" to the Book through our perseverance and assiduity in lectio, then we will comprehend the folly of the good God.

20. To know Christ crucified, we must be crucified to the world.

21. "Here I am; may God write in me what he wills," said Mary. When the heart is a letter written by God, all of God's letters resound in the heart.

22. When we live the Good News we offer the world reasons to live and die.

~ *First Movement* ~

23. *Lectio Divina* is:

• A meditated reading, above all of the Bible, prolonged in contemplative prayer.

• A reading about God with the eyes of a spouse and the heart of the Church.

• A reading gratuitously made in order to gratuitously receive the Author of grace.

• A transformative reading that evangelizes us, makes us evangelizers.

• An interpersonal relationship in faith and love, with Christ who speaks to us, in the Spirit who teaches us, and under the gaze of the Father who regards us.

• A pilgrimage of words towards the Mystery of the Word.

• A slow assimilation of saving Truth while in dialogue with the Savior.

• An enamored faith that seeks the Face of God in order to anticipate what is yearned for.

• Immersion, conpenetration, divinization, emersion.

24. *Lectio* is *divina*

• for God is read in this Word and with his Spirit.

• because we are brought before the Mystery, and it is made present in the heart.

• when God who speaks is heard and his presence tasted.

25. Because *Lectio Divina* is dialogue, it is therefore reception, self-gift, and communion. Reception by attention and reflection, self-gift through our response, communion through encounter.

26. Miriam of Nazareth, in dialogue with Gabriel, offers us a captivating example of *Lectio vere divina*.

27. Because *Lectio Divina* is life, it is also movement. Movement in that different moments or experiences can be discerned: reading, meditation, prayer, contemplation.

28. Reading, meditation, prayer, contemplation . . . is what normally occurs when we give it time to happen.

29. The gratuity of *Lectio Divina* is different from the utility of study. Study endeavors to master the word, *Lectio Divina* surrenders and yields before it.

30. *Lectio Divina* also differs from spiritual reading. The latter can have as its end the acquisition of knowledge, the formulation of convictions, or the stimulus for generous self-giving. The aim of the former is union with God in faith and love.

∾ Second Movement ∾

31. *Lectio Divina* is not, as a rule, immediately gratifying. It is an active and passive process of long duration. One does not reap the day following the sowing! The worm is not instantly transformed into a butterfly!

32. There is nothing as purifying as enduring the silence of the Word. But all who know how to wait reap the reward.

33. If you allow yourself to be possessed by the Word, you will hear even his silence.

34. In *Lectio Divina* there is also room for the Fathers of the Church and Citeaux; their writings confirm and amplify the biblical message. Because of their Christian spirit they are sure guides of correct interpretation, and by their holiness of life they teach us how to live and help us to commune in Holy Spirit.

35. Other books are helpful in the measure that they allow us to assimilate the Mystery and be transformed by it.

36. When the beginner says, "For me, everything is *Lectio Divina*," it is to be understood that for that one *Lectio Divina* is meaningless.

∼ *Third Movement* ∼

37. Pay attention: it is God who wishes to speak to you and who awaits your reply.

38. The various experiences of *Lectio Divina* come together in one movement of the Spirit. They can coexist and mutually overlap; they even alternate in an ever-changing order. The pedestrian makes many movements, but all come together in one action: walking.

39. Assiduous practice lessens rigidity. Those who exercise little increase rigidity and make slow progress. Those who do not exercise do not advance.

40. *Lectio Divina* is a daily practice at a privileged hour, all the time that is necessary to bring about a dialogue with the most faithful of friends.

Reading

41. Reading is a form of listening that allows a way of always being able to return to what was heard. And listening is being and letting be. Without listening there is no interpersonal relationship.

42. If you read to read and not to have read, then your reading is serene, restful, and disinterested.

43. Do not waste time in looking for a text that is pleasing. Choose your text beforehand, perhaps the day's liturgical readings, or follow some theme or a consecutive reading of the whole Bible.

44. The fool falls into the temptation of saying, "I already know this text!" The wise one knows that it is one thing to know the chemical formula of water and another to savor it by a spring on a summer's day.

45. If you do not comprehend what you are reading, ask the Lord to help you to understand. And you help the Lord by this: if you read the text in its context, compare it with parallel texts, find key words, determine the central message.

46. If you have read well, you will be able to say what the text means.

Meditation

47. To meditate is to chew and ruminate, for it is to reflect, remember, interpret, penetrate. One who thus meditates on the Word is transformed according to the Word and becomes a mediator of the Word.

48. If the text read means nothing to you, love the Word beyond the words and do not hesitate to surrender yourself without reserve. And if the text is a hard saying and you apply it to your neighbor, try rereading it in the first person.

49. There is no meditation without distraction. Return, then, to the reading. Concentrate on the key words.

50. When the text speaks to your heart, you have reached and received a precious fruit of meditation.

Prayer

51. Prayer during *Lectio Divina* can take many forms: praise, petition, thanksgiving, compunction . . .

52. Having listened by reading and meditation, you can now speak in prayer. If you know what the text says and what the text says to you, what do you say to him?

53. Silence can also be a response, as much for the one who prays, carried out of himself, as for him who knows all.

Contemplation

54. To contemplate is to take silent delight in the Temple that is the Risen Christ.

55. To contemplate is to encounter the Word, beyond words.

56. To contemplate is to live in the Risen One, rooted in the NOW of this earth, reaching out to the beyond of the heavens.

57. Contemplation is vision. The contemplative sees the resurrection in the cross, life in death, the Risen One in the Crucified.

58. Contemplation is the thirst caused by the seeming absence of the satiety of mutual presence.

59. The contemplative is at a loss for words, simply because he or she knows.

~ *Fourth Movement* ~

Collatio

60. *Collatio* is contribution or provision, confrontation or dialogue. It is to provide fuel for meditation, fire for prayer, light for contemplation, motivation for acts.

Action

61. Action refers, before all, to the conversion of one's heart, behaving as a disciple and under the discipline of the Truth for our salvation.

Collaboration

62. Every good work is in collaboration with the One who does all things well. He who collaborates with him works and prays with all.

∽ *Postlude* ∽

63. The Bible is not intended only to tell us about God but to transform us according to the form of Christ.

64. Scripture is the word that informs, giving us the form of Christians.

65. The virginal conception by the Virgin Mother is a mystery of redemption and also a model for imitation: conceiving the Word in the womb of the heart, embracing the will of the Father, makes us brother, sister, and mother.

66. The Word and the words are for us and not us for the words, because we are for the Word.

67. Those who have progressed in *Lectio Divina* experience the need for fewer words and more of the Word.

68. Those who have been transformed by the Word can read it in the events of each day, and in those signs of the times that are voices of God manifested through the deepest human aspirations.

69. Those who have revealed truth engraved in the innermost depths of their hearts do not depend on the Sacred Text and are for others a living Bible.

70. If you want to know and reach Christ, you will arrive much sooner by following him than by reading about him.

Select Bibliography

Bernard of Clairvaux. *The Works of Bernard of Clairvaux*. Translated by Michael Casey, et al. Cistercian Fathers Series. Kalamazoo, Mich.: Cistercian Publications, 1969.

Casey, Michael. *Sacred Reading: The Ancient Art of Lectio Divina*. Liguori, Mo.: Triumph Books, 1995.

Cummings, Charles. *Monastic Practices*. Cistercian Studies Series. Kalamazoo, Mich.: Cistercian Publications, 1986.

Downey, Michael. *Living in the Land of Desire*. Mahwah, N.J.: Paulist Press, 1997.

Hall, Thelma. *Too Deep for Words*. Mahwah, N.J.: Paulist Press, 1988.

Illich, Ivan. *In the Vineyard of the Text: A Commentary to Hugh's Didascalion*. Chicago: The University of Chicago Press, 1993.

Keating, Thomas. *Intimacy with God*. New York: Crossroad, 1994.

Leclercq, Jean. *Love of Learning and the Desire for God*. Cistercian Studies Series 105. Kalamazoo, Mich.: Cistercian Publications, 1990.

Merton, Thomas. *Opening the Bible*. Collegeville, Minn.: The Liturgical Press, 1970.

Mulholland, Robert. *Shaped by the Word: The Power of Sacred Scripture in Spiritual Formation*. Nashville, Tenn.: The Upper Room, 1985.

Muto, Susan. *A Practical Guide to Spiritual Reading.* Danville, N.J.: Dimension Books, 1976.

Pennington, M. Basil. *Awake in the Spirit.* New York: Crossroad, 1993.

———. *The Cistercians.* Collegeville, Minn.: The Liturgical Press, 1992.

———. *Daily We Touch Him.* 2d ed. Kansas City, Kan.: Sheed and Ward, 1997.

———. *Lessons from the Monastery That Touch Your Life.* Mahwah, N.J.: Paulist Press, 1994.

———. *Monastic Life: A Short History of Monasticism and Its Spirit.* Petersham, Mass.: St. Bede's Publications, 1989.

———. *The Monastic Way.* New York: Crossroad, 1990.

Peter of Celles. *Selected Works.* Translated by Hugh Feiss. Cistercian Studies Series. Kalamazoo, Mich.: Cistercian Publications, 1987.

William of St. Thierry. *The Works of William of St. Thierry.* Translated by Penelope Lawson, et al. Cistercian Fathers Series. Kalamazoo, Mich.: Cistercian Publications, 1969.

Van Kaam, Adrian. *The Woman at the Well.* Danville, N.J.: Dimension Books, 1976.

OF RELATED INTEREST

Thomas Keating
INTIMACY WITH GOD
Practical ways to find oneness with God and everyone
else through a contemplative lifestyle.
0-8245-1588-9, $16.95 paperback

Thomas Keating
AWAKENINGS
An examination of the key events in the ministry of
Jesus, the important parables, and the many celebra-
tions of his presence in light of today's experience
of living.
0-8245-1044-5, $12.95 paperback

Please support your local bookstore,
or call 1-800-395-0690.
For a free catalog, please write us at
THE CROSSROAD PUBLISHING COMPANY
481 EIGHTH AVENUE, SUITE 1550
NEW YORK, NY 10001

crossroad

OF RELATED INTEREST

OF RELATED INTEREST

Dick Ryan, Editor
STRAIGHT FROM THE HEART
Reflections from Twentieth Century Mystics
A collection of wise sayings, profound proverbs, and
deep wisdom on a variety of spiritual themes from the
best-known mystics of the 20th century, including Joyce
Rupp, Henri Nouwen, Miriam Therese Winter and
Thomas Merton.
0-8245-1923-X; $19.95 hardcover

Simon Parke
ORIGINS
For Those Bored with the Shallow End
"When profound, intelligent, and witty go together, you
know you have someone worth listening to! This wonderful collection of quick, readable 'parables' will stay
with you for a long time-and lead you out of the
shallows." - RICHARD ROHR, O.F.M.
0-8245-1910-8; $16.95 hardcover

Please support your local bookstore,
or call 1-800-395-0690.
For a free catalog, please write us at
THE CROSSROAD PUBLISHING COMPANY
481 EIGHTH AVENUE, SUITE 1550
NEW YORK, NY 10001

crossroad

Of Related Interest

—■—

Robert Kirschner
DIVINE THINGS
Seeking the Sacred in a Secular Age
"Kirschner's lively, up-to-date and wonderfully rich
presentation of the ancient wisdom of the Hebrew
Scriptures will enliven and enlighten the lives of all
readers." - M. BASIL PENNINGTON, O.C.S.O.
0-8245-1897-7; $14.95 paperback

Susanna Tamaro
TURNING HOME
A Memoir
Tamaro's shy, rebellious voice shines through every
page of this sensitive memoir. Having grown up in Italy
near one of the bloodiest battlefields of the world wars,
she looks unblinkingly at the reality of evil, only to find
the Spirit of a loving God touching her heart.
0-8245-1902-7; $14.95 paperback

—■—

Please support your local bookstore,
or call 1-800-395-0690.
For a free catalog, please write us at
THE CROSSROAD PUBLISHING COMPANY
481 EIGHTH AVENUE, SUITE 1550
NEW YORK, NY 10001

crossroad

Of Related Interest

———■———

Jean Fournee
Praying the Angelus
These recent years have seen a renewal of interest in
the prayer of the Angelus. This book outlines the ori-
gins and history of the evolution and development of
this prayer. It is the first study published on
this subject.
0-8245-1864-0; $8.95 paperback

Robert Barron
Heaven in Stone and Glass
Experiencing the Spirituality of the Great Cathedrals
This book combines both meditation and Christian art.
Lovers of the sacred space created by Gothic cathedrals
will revel in the spirit in which they were built.
Christians interested in deepening their faith will find
much nourishment as they ponder the depth of faith in
God which is carved into the very stone cathedrals.
0-8245-1863-2; $16.95 hardcover

———■———

Please support your local bookstore,
or call 1-800-395-0690.
For a free catalog, please write us at
THE CROSSROAD PUBLISHING COMPANY
481 EIGHTH AVENUE, SUITE 1550
NEW YORK, NY 10001

crossroad